May it be delightful my house;
From my head may it be delightful;
To my feet may it be delightful;
Where I lie may it be delightful;
All above me may it be delightful;
All around me may it be delightful.

A GIFT
TO
THE STREET

Photographs by
Carol Olwell

Commentary by
Judith Lynch Waldhorn

Antelope Island Press
1976

Ms. Waldhorn's research for the text of this book was supported by a grant from the National Endowment for the Arts in Washington, D.C., a Federal agency.

The drawings of balloon frame construction and the five Victorian house types were done by Stephen Rynerson.

Production handled by Richard Schuettge.

Design by Carol Olwell and Dominic Di Mare.

Type set in Aldus and Cloister by Holbrook Teter at Spring Creek Typesetting in Healdsburg.

Mechanicals made by Hal Hershey at Fifth Street Design in Berkeley.

Camera and press work done by Wolf Schaefer at Phelps/Schaefer Litho-Graphics Co. in San Francisco.

Binding was done by Vince Mullins and his family at Cardoza-James Bindery in San Francisco.

Published in the United States by Antelope Island Press,
P.O. Box 31508, San Francisco, California, 94131.

First Printing September 1976
Second Printing November 1976

Library of Congress Cataloguing in Publication Data

Olwell, Carol, 1944-
    A gift to the street.

    Includes bibliographical references and index.
    1.   Architecture, Domestic — California — San Francisco.
2.   Architecture, Victorian — San Francisco.   3.   Architecture,
Victorian — United States.   I.   Waldhorn, Judith Lynch.   II.   Title.
NA7238.S35048   728.3   76-26576

ISBN 0-917946-01-4

3

Preface

Victorian architecture has been out of favor with the official architectural establishment for more than 75 years. But it has never been totally out of favor with the people who live in and pass by these structures day in and day out.

The decoration that the Victorians applied to their buildings has been decried as "useless ornamentation" by the architectural tastemakers of our time. Victorian houses don't have the "purity" of form and function that modern architecture demands.

Yet I for one am tired of a modern architecture that preaches at me and attempts to uplift me morally. I am ready for an architecture that is entertaining — or even amusing. Which is why I am a closet Victorian.

The Victorian house builders consciously set out to make houses that were "beautiful." To them, ornamentation and decoration were an integral part of beauty. In this belief, they were drawing on a building tradition that began long before the ancient Greeks. It is only in the short span of the 20th century that designers have relentlessly stripped away every vestige of ornament and decoration from buildings — both when constructing new or when "remodelling" the old.

Ornamentation and structural variety on Victorian houses provide a visual richness that has proved, over the years, pleasing to people. Brackets, spindles, decorative shingles, oriels and bays, sawn wood ornaments, verge boards, tiles, etched and stained glass, incised ornament, appliques, soaring chimneys — there were literally hundreds of design variations and materials that the Victorian builder could use to make a house "beautiful" — and distinctive from others in the same architectural style. With pattern books and architectural parts catalogues, even an unimaginative builder could create a dwelling that we find amazing today. On a streetscape, Victorian houses provide a variety of related patterns, textures, highlights and shadows that most people find, on a deep emotional level, satisfying and enriching .

Adding to the public's current re-evaluation of the legacy of the Victorian builders is the sad realization that buildings this rich in detail will never be built again. Worse, neglect and the bulldozer have been taking a terrible toll of the Victorian houses that remain.

San Francisco has a particularly fanciful and unique collection of carpenter-built houses. Fortunately, many people have come to realize what a precious legacy it is. Many of the beautiful old Victorians have been restored to their former elegance. And the visual environment of the entire city is better off for it.

This phenomenon is not unique to San Francisco, thankfully. All over America people are looking at Victorian houses with a fresh perspective, as *A Gift to the Street* will show. The recently despised architectural embellishments are being re-discovered as delights for the eye and the spirit. And they are being lovingly restored.

Our generation is only the caretaker for this wonderful legacy of unique architecture. Happily, more and more people are discovering what a joy it can be to preserve this heritage from a bygone era. Our descendants will thank us for it.

Brooklyn, N.Y.   Clem Labine, Editor
April 26, 1976   The Old-House Journal

Contents

v PREFACE

x LETTER TO THE READER

xiii A VICTORIAN . . . .

GIFTS TO THE STREETS

2 HOUSES WITH FLAT FRONTS

8 DOORWAYS

16 WINDOWS

22 HOUSES WITH SLANTED BAYS

32 DECORATIVE IRON

40 HOUSES WITH SQUARE BAYS

52 FLORAL DECORATIVES

62 COLUMNS

72 HOUSES WITH TOWERS

80 STAINED GLASS

88 FACES

98 HOUSES WITH GABLES

106 NEWEL POSTS

120 SUNBURSTS

130 EXTRAORDINARY DETAILS

144 PLANS & PATTERNS

163 WHAT ABOUT STYLES?

171 PELTON'S CHEAP DWELLINGS

173 "WHAT IS PAST IS PROLOGUE"

APPENDIX

178 BALLOON FRAME CONSTRUCTION

180 FLAT FRONT ITALIANATE

181 ITALIANATE WITH SLANTED BAY

182 QUEEN ANNE TOWER HOUSE

183 SAN FRANCISCO STICK

184 QUEEN ANNE ROWHOUSE

185 STREET LISTING BY PHOTOGRAPH NUMBER

188 ALPHABETICAL STREET LISTING

191 INDEX

192 ILLUSTRATION SOURCES

193 REFERENCES

194 ACKNOWLEDGMENTS

To My Family

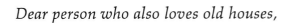

Dear person who also loves old houses,

    I suppose this book began with the house where my grandfather was born in 1888, shown on the preceding page. Built in 1870, purchased by his father in 1885, the house became a warm and hospitable family center for three generations. It was demolished in 1945, to make way for a medical office building. Somehow I always thought that office building could have been located just as well on the corner across the street. On that corner another beautiful old house had been torn down in 1935, to make way for a gas station.

    Be that as it may, for my great grandfather this house was a step up from the days when he used to drive a stage coach for Wells Fargo. For my grandfather it was home, and for me it lives only in photographs and the memories of my mother and grandmother.

    But I suppose it was this house, or the stories of it, that filtered down through my childhood experiences to a quiet place inside, where things that should not have been violated are kept. Perhaps that's why, when watching old houses being demolished in San Francisco years later, it always seemed faintly reminiscent of an elderly person being viciously mauled and attacked. At any rate I was troubled by the "wholesale slaughter", if you will, of neighborhoods in San Francisco in the name of redevelopment. When some money was left to me (ironically by that same arm of the family that had chosen to tear down the house), it seemed best to use it to document, street by street, what was left.

My study was neither preceded by nor based on architectural or historical knowledge of Victorian architecture. Rather it was motivated by a purely visual delight in what I saw. I tried to photograph the old houses as they were seen by the people who lived in and with them, complete with telephone poles, wires, and the ever present automobile. Often it was clear to me what ought to be photographed and what not; but in those cases where the house was in very bad shape, or on the borderline of the Victorian era, I was guided by five questions that I would ask of the house. Are you old? Are you beautiful? Are you unique? Do I like you anyway? (I've never been one for too much discipline . . . .) Will somebody besides me miss you when you're gone? If I could answer yes to at least two of these, there would be a click and a shuffle on down the street. Such was the procedure through two years and 11,000 photographs. Only a small fraction of that study could be included here; indeed this book barely touches upon what there is to see.

As I worked it became increasingly important to me to pay a tribute to the old houses — a tribute that did not ask for the past, but stated what they give to the present. In that light, text in the photographic section has been kept to a minimum, so that the houses may speak for themselves.

But why am I so fond of these buildings? Because such houses as these will never be built on earth again. Because they are often both handsome and lovely, slightly irrational, and always a visual feast. Because their very presence was and is, day in and day out, a gift to every neighbor, postman and passerby on the street. Because they are large, public reflections of qualities to be found in each of us. Walk down a street, and you'll find a house that borders on the puritanical, next to one that is playful, next to one that is pompous and affected, next door to one that is straightforward and bold. And all are covered with sensuous details.

In essence then, I see the old houses as unique, public, large-scale celebrations of life, worthy of preservation and respect. This book is being offered to you in that spirit.

Fondly,
Carol

6

A Victorian...

It's a private kind of discovery. You might spy a cameo face winking over a doorway or respond to a rowhouse rhythm as the sun glints on ten bay windows. Perhaps you wonder what decorations adorned an old house now disfigured by asbestos shingles or smothered with stucco. Once you begin to notice, a flood of delerious details will engulf your eyes. You see the similarities: the narrow city lot, the ranks of plaster garlands, the brave false fronts. Yet assembled on their faces is an inexhaustible variety of expressions, clues to the language of their builders. Look there, the peaked roof is punctuated, its finial is an exclamation point!

Stand in front of a home and look closely. Was it carved from a big block of wood by a whittler with a sharp knife? No, its redwood pieces were machine produced, ordered from millshop catalogues, and placed on the house fronts in a jigsaw puzzle, its joinings and edges hidden by coats of paint.

Two forces helped shape Victorian America: the architect who designed unique homes for clients, such as illustration 1, and the merchant-builder who purchased multiple lots and constructed rows of homes identical in plan, varied in detail, with only minor choices open to the prospective buyer. *A Gift to the Street* celebrates the contribution

Illustration 1

of both professions, whose ornate mansions and simpler rowhouses remind us of a slower, more decorative time.

Discovery of Victorians is not enough; as Robert Frost explained, it must "begin in delight and end in wisdom."[1] The eye's delight stirs the mind to wonderment: How were the houses built? Where did the ideas originate? Who made the millwork; who devised its almost infinite combinations? To answer these questions, the celebration in this book takes two forms: first, photographs of Victorian homes and details, and second, a text section which explores new historical sources. Some prefer to enjoy the houses just by gazing at them; others prefer to learn the vocabulary of details first. For them, pages 180-184 are a Victorian anatomy lesson, with drawings and details of five varieties.

San Francisco's 1906 earthquake and fire destroyed many examples of the work of the Victorian architect. Most city building documents also perished, leaving too many of our carpenter-built homes anonymous, undated and unclaimed. Yet most of the Victorians which survived are in clusters of identical homes, cottages & flats which are the entrepreneurial echo of the merchant builder. In the text and photographs of *A Gift to the Street*, you will learn to read the language of the Victorian millwright in the archives of his work. There clues survive as "signature details," the special twist of standard millwork which made it the personal statement of the carpenter-builder.

Repeated throughout the book is the theme we have chosen to symbolize these anonymous builders, the cast iron circle within a square found embedded in the sidewalk in front of many homes. This grate served two purposes: It vented sewer gas, and it advertised the early builders and suppliers who left at our feet a map of the Victorian times. Those all but forgotten calling cards are their footprints; follow these humble sidewalk plates to receive *A Gift to the Street*.

GIFTS TO

THE STREETS

HOUSES WITH

FLAT FRONTS

9

Many San Francisco homes built during the 1870's had flat fronts, with high false cornices added, they say, to make the houses look bigger and more impressive. Look behind the false front; you will find the real peaked roof. Now we call these buildings 'flat-front Italianates,' although that name was not used by their builders.

The hoods over the doorways and windows are wooden copies of stone motifs used in earlier times. Some of these flat-fronted buildings are edged with beveled blocks; these 'quoins' are wooden replicas of bricks or stones used to reinforce the corners of castles or fortresses.

In each photographic section, we share some informal thoughts about the houses and their details. To learn more about the architectural details mentioned, please turn to the Appendix to see drawings of five San Francisco Victorian varieties with all parts labeled. Underneath each photograph is a number; in the Appendix, street addresses are listed by this photograph number and alphabetically.

10

11

12

13

14

DOORWAYS

18

19

An entrance may be spindled or bracketed. It may open in columned formality or welcome you with a casual yawn. Hundreds of kinds of doors were listed in millshop catalogues all over the country, and their designs were changed often to keep pace with new fashions in house plans. The Niehaus Brothers in Berkeley, California, offered many varieties, as shown in text illustration 31. Some doors came in double sets; the outer pair swings inward to form a decorative vestibule.

Victorians who bought tract houses were often given a choice of front doors. From Fernando Nelson, who is described in the text section, you might choose the 'plain' door for $1.25 or splurge on a 'fancy' one for $5. One year Nelson's $5 door looked like the ones shown here which have six round buttons in the middle and a sunburst on the bottom panel. Many front doors still have panes of stained or colored glass. When the sun shines through, their hallways glow!

20

21

22

23

24

25

26

27

28

29

30

31

32

33

14

34

35

WINDOWS

37

Windows and their surrounding decorations were also a target for a wide variety of millwork combinations. In the 1870's and early 1880's, many windows were topped by hoods of different shapes, such as the triangular pediment, the 'squeezed' pediment, or the hood which was a 'segment' of an arc. Sometimes the windows and door treatments matched; other times the builders and architects mixed shapes freely.

The window panes themselves were often shaped, sometimes to echo the squeezed, arched, flat, or segmented hoods. Some main clear panels were edged with small colored ones. Red with yellow and blue with green were frequent combinations. Later in the era, builders chose flatter, more geometric millwork to outline their windows, as ornament and fashion kept pace with new machinery for the manufacture of embellishment.

38

39

40

41

42

43

44

45

46

47

48

49

50

51

21

HOUSES WITH
SLANTED BAYS

54

The bay window may have originated to provide more light, better cross-ventilation, or additional floor space. But perhaps the most plausible explanation was given by an architect of the time who wrote that the bay window gave him additional space to add embellishment to a house. The homes shown in this section all have bays which slant; three sides form a polygonal protrusion from the main house front.

The bay window was so embraced by San Francisco builders, such as the man who built the cluster shown above, that some people called it "the city of bay windows." Versions of bay windowed homes built in the 1870's, such as the house which begins this section, have details also found on flat-front Italianates: columns, false fronts, brackets, quoins, and window hoods. By the mid-1880's, these simpler wooden replicas of stone ornaments were further enriched by an explosion of detail in many new patterns. The last photograph in this section, and the sets of bay window tops, middles, and bottoms, show this transition in decoration.

56

57

58

59

60

61

62

63

27

66

67

69

68

70

71

73

72

74

DECORATIVE IRON

During the Victorian era, decorative iron was a common item
in the repertoire of both builders and architects. As the house plans
in the text section show, most homes were topped by a row of
ironwork, often in the shape of spears or arrows. Since this ironwork
provided a space to walk on the roof and perhaps use a spyglass
to watch for ships at sea, some people call it a 'captain's walk'
or a 'widow's walk.' The photograph on pages viii-ix shows the ironwork which used to guard most rooftops; you may still find it over
doorways.

Virtually all of this iron cresting is gone from the roofs and
the porticoes of San Francisco. Some was removed because it made
the roof leak; the rest fell victim to modernizations or to wartime
scrap metal drives.

Though roofs and doorways were shorn, much decorative iron
is still intact, as in the fences, gates, and handrails shown here.
The arrowhead and the spearpoint are important themes, perhaps
to echo the bristling rooflines. Circles, floral patterns, hearts, and
spirals are there, too, intertwined with fleurs-de-lis in a lacy barrier
whose fragility belies its strength.

78

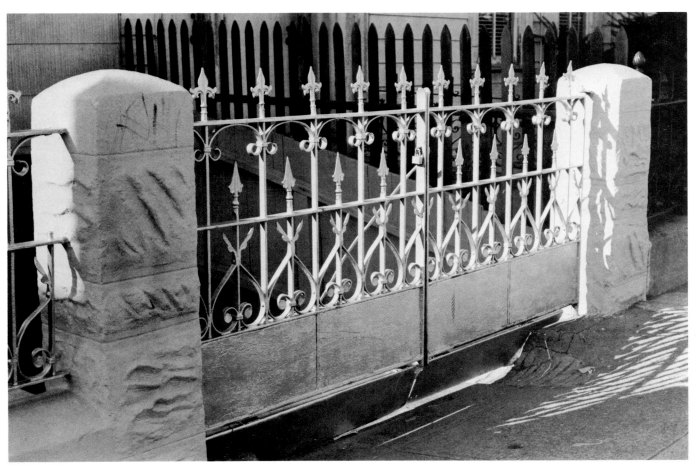

79

35

80

81

36

82

83

84

85

37

86

87

88

89

90

39

HOUSES WITH

SQUARE BAYS

The square bay succeeded the slanted one in the 1880's, as house plans began to emphasize a more massive vertical home laden with wooden products of the millwork machine age.

The houses have other characteristic details besides the square bays. Many had false gables, like a triangular version of the false front, shown in the cluster above. Other homes were topped by a 'Mansard,' or French, roof cap. Most square bayed homes originally had either false gables or French caps, but many have been removed by overzealous modernizers.

Some houses with square bays were built in identical rows; other builders made slight variations within clusters. The two shown at the right are next-door neighbors. Notice how the false gable and its crowning finial make the house above look different from its virtually identical neighbor.

93

94

95

96

97

98

99

100

101

102

103

104

107

108

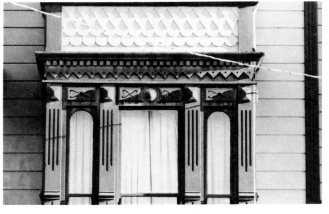

109

110

111

112

113

114

115

116

117

The windows shown above and to the left offer a brief glimpse
into the bewildering variety of embellishments available to builders.
These wooden decorations could be ordered in great quantities from
local mills, whose annual catalogues offered hundreds of variations.
Some builders and architects chose from amongst the standard
offerings; others brought in their own designs to be manufactured.

Many adopted certain millwork items and combinations as
their own special signature details. The person who built the house
shown above used swags underneath the roofline and also applied
shield-shaped decoratives with jig-sawn fleurs-de-lis. He used a
set of five small embellishments, three anchors and two buttons,
under each set of bay windows. His signature details are shown
on the next two pages; he built homes like these in at least six clusters
in three neighborhoods. Many other builders and architects also
used signature details, particularly in the 1880's and 1890's, when
a wide variety of house parts were available to be chosen and combined
at will. These decorative clues may help you discover the date and
identity of an old house.

118

119

FLORAL

DECORATIVES

Nature was a favorite decorative theme of the Victorians, who used buds, petals, flowers, vines, and leaves lavishly inside and outside their homes. These themes appear indoors on wallpaper, borders and wainscotting. Some Victorian furniture is garnished with flowers, and the corner blocks of the framework around a doorway may also hold a rosebud.

Some of these representations of nature look like inspired products of delicate individual handcrafting. Yet they were almost all made by machines, as Victorians used mass production to assist in their celebration of the natural. The fragile-looking flower which introduces this section was actually stamped from a block of damp wood by three hundred pounds of pressure from a hydraulic press.

Look carefully; even in the shadow of a fire escape, you may spy a floral pattern. It may be sawn, pressed, or turned from wood, molded from sawdust or cast in plaster or metal. Some are carved in a realistic manner; others are more stylized. Even a basement ventilator plate may host an abstract pattern of leaves and vines. These floral decoratives were not always soothing and innocent; the leaves in the last photograph of this section glare at us menacingly like untrimmed eyebrows.

123

124

125

126

127

128

130

129

131

132

133

COLUMNS

135

136

Victorian house part catalogues offered columns of "any size or shape," and they were used in abundance. Look for columns in entryways, in verandas, cut in half as pilasters and, in miniature, as colonnettes to outline bay windows. The column shaft might be of solid or hollow wood, or it might be made of cast metal. Some columns have decorative capitals which echo earlier classical motifs: the acanthus leaves of the Corinthian capital, the spiraled Ionic capital, or the two combined into a Composite. The shaft may be beaded, fluted, or plain. The column base may be the bulbous tulip shown above, or the chaste incised pattern shown on the right.

    Millwrights of the era soon moved past these classical themes and began to construct their own versions of columns. Some borrowed from the Egyptian, some were geometric, and others were composed of four columns flanked by a pair of pilasters which frame the door.

138

139

140

141

142

143

144

145

146

147

148

149

150

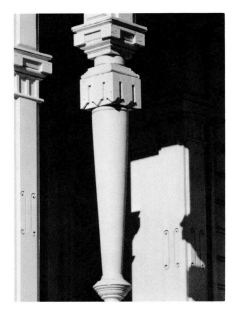

151

152

153

154

Some builders made the portico columns part of their vocabulary of signature details. Fernando Nelson, who built the homes shown above and at the right, often turned his columns on a lathe from a massive piece of redwood. Instead of a classical capital, he added some lengths of dowels and balls sawn in half and applied to look like dripping paint. Nelson himself called this detail "drips." Over the entryway of some of his homes, between the columns, he placed the jigsawn "O's" which are another of his trademarks, called "donuts." His straightforward names for details simply reflected the way the pieces of assembled wood looked to him. Both the donuts and the drips were invented by Nelson and manufactured "by the barrel" at the Townley Brothers, a San Francisco millshop.

155

156

HOUSES WITH TOWERS

157

Oone of the first west coast house plans with a tower was published
in San Francisco in 1884. But much earlier an English architect
summed up his reasons for adding a tower to a house: "A tower
or lofty belvedere is a pleasing addition, to command an extensive
and varied prospect. It affords an opportunity to the ladies
of the family to accompany the sportsmen in their chase,
with their eyes, if not more Amazonially on horseback. It can
enable the inmates of such a watch tower to espy the approach
of any unbidden, unwanted visitors — of any bores, for
instance . . . . A bookstand and a harp would suffice to render
such a place a delightful snuggery, a kind of aerial boudoir,
equally fitted for speculation or meditation."[2]

158

159

160

161

162

164

165

166

167

168

STAINED GLASS

171

Color was an important element of Victorian decoration, and by the 1880's, different kinds of colored glass were widely available. It was used everywhere, to edge a clear skylight, to sparkle in hallways, as entry transoms, or as small panels over bay windows. Those shown above wink out of a home whose plaster looks out of focus. That blur is caused by its recent 'modernization' with a textured spray coating which tends to obliterate detail.

An 1884 architectural magazine described different methods of colored glass manufacture. In mosaic windows, such as most of those in this section, each piece of glass is a different color, making up a pattern which may be either abstract or floral. The pattern is created because each piece of glass is separated from the others by a thin piece of leading.

Some windows combine leaded, stained glass with another technique, enameling. The faces in the centers of two of the windows shown at the right are painted directly on with a brush, rather than made up of separate pieces. The subject of these portraits may be well known, such as the two composers. But sometimes a home-owner would glorify herself with an enameled portrait over the entry transom.

172

173

174

175

84

176

177

85

178

179

180

181

FACES

182

Look closely at the photographs above and on the opposite page. Can you discover the faces peering at you? The faces of men and women, and of gods and demons, were a favorite form of decoration during the Victorian age. Through these faces, the homes and their designers may express human qualities; a house may be bold or shy, playful or reserved, homey or pompous.

Many faces and other small decorations are being discovered anew by careful restorers, who work patiently for hours scraping away dirt and layers of old paint with a dental pick. They are often rewarded by the welcoming smiles of a shy maiden or the grimaces of a gape-jawed gargoyle. These creatures were usually made of plaster, but sometimes wood, cast iron, or zinc was used. These facial adornments were most prevalent in the 1890's, when plaster embellishments were in vogue and widely available.

Once you start to notice, you will find faces everywhere, tucked into a transom, glaring from a gable, pouting over a portico, capping a column or presiding over a pediment.

184

185

186

187

188

189

190

191

192

193

HOUSES WITH GABLES

195

During the 1890's, houses with gables began their peaked-roof march over San Francisco's hills. Inside the gable was an attic, which Victorian builders used to offer yet another option to their customers. Home buyers could order the attic finished for an extra bedroom, or left unfinished for future expansion. These homes have the same decorative motifs and the same basic shape as the towered houses shown earlier, but the turret was left off when tract builders began to produce clusters of Queen Anne rowhouses.

The triangle of the gable offered yet another target for adornment. Changes in texture were indicated by combining different shingle shapes, as shown in the following series. In others, you may find sunbursts, floral decoratives, a brace, spindles, the plaster garlands called 'rinceaux,' or even a double gable. Notice the way Victorian builders attached the peaked roof to the slanted bay window: two brackets smooth the joining, finished with a bulbous hanging pendant or drop. In some gabled houses, the eaves are further dressed with a wide bargeboard, or vergeboard, itself the site of even more decoration.

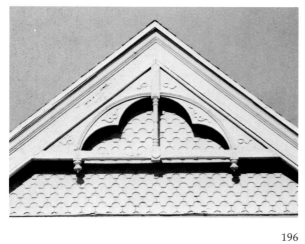

196

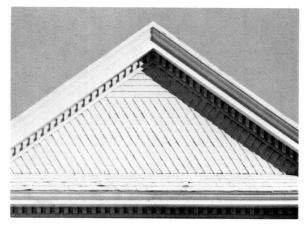

197

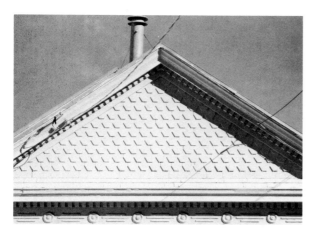

198

199

200

202

203

204

205

206

207

209

NEWEL POSTS

Indoors and out, the newel post forms a staunch ending to a flight of stairs, with its balusters and its handrail swooping up to a door or a landing. Newels occupied many pages in Victorian mill catalogues; turn to text illustration 31 to see some of the newels offered by a local shop.

Newel posts are made in different ways and carry varied embellishments. Look at the photograph above. The post on the left is intact, but the one on the right has been sawn in half, perhaps by an angry neighbor. This fortuitous bisection lets us look directly into the heart of the newel to see how it was made.

211

212

213

214

215

216

The newel post above was formed on a lathe, a millworking machine which turns squared pieces of wood into rounded ones. As the wood spins around, the millwright uses cutting tools to shape it. This post also has buttons, those small round pieces which are also turned on the lathe and which may show up anywhere, from the newel post to the gable. Some newels were constructed, others are notched, with sections sawn off the corners. Many newels have a lathe-turned finial applied on top.

Balusters are the small posts which support the handrail. They are also an important decorative part of the stair system and may duplicate, complement or form a counterpoint to the main newel post. Most balusters are turned on a lathe, but occasionally you may see simple beaded square ones or flat sawn ones.

217

218

219

220

221

222

223

224

225

226

227

228

229

230

231

232

233

234

236

237

238

239

240

243

242

244

245

246

247

SUNBURSTS

249

250

What is the origin of these beaming suns? Are they rising or setting? Some say they represent the buoyant optimism of the Victorian era; others say it is the sun which never set on the once farflung British Empire. Whatever their roots, sunbursts are ideal decoratives for anywhere on a house surface, because their rays can stretch out into the broadest gable or squeeze into the tiniest pediment. They are most often found on homes of wood, a material which is easily worked into many shapes.

Doors, gates, window hoods, entryways, or arches may all sport sunbursts, and their rays may have many shapes. Some are beveled, others are flat and stylized, while other rays have softened curves. Some have incised decorations which look like wriggling worms. Some rays overlap and could be folded up like a fan. Their sunny faces cheer us in the gloomiest weather.

252

251

253

254

255

256

257

258

259

260

262

EXTRAORDINARY

DETAILS

264

The house which leads this section is noteworthy for its owls, who keep a watchful eye on passing neighbors. Yet these owls are but one example of the imaginative freedom expressed in the exuberant embellishment of the Victorian era. The old houses are appealing because they, like ourselves, possess both masculine and feminine characteristics.

Look closely at the floral decoratives, finials, pendants, columns, newel posts, and other sawn and turned parts. You will notice many details which are highly suggestive of human anatomy. The often-used button, applied freely to gables, newels, windows and almost every other available bare surface, looks much like a navel. The examples shown here are not unusual; something similar can be discovered on almost every Victorian house.

Whether these details sprang from repressed desires or from a robust sense of life is neither our task nor our intent to decide. It is important simply to realize that the parts are there and that they contribute in a subtle way to the personal nature of the homes. We offer this section on extraordinary details as an invitation to become aware and appreciative of how the essence of Victorian architecture mirrors human nature in its attempt to attract, please and delight.

265

266

268

269

270

271

272

273

274

275

277

278

279

280

281

282

283

R A PRIVATE RESIDENCE.

Illustration 2

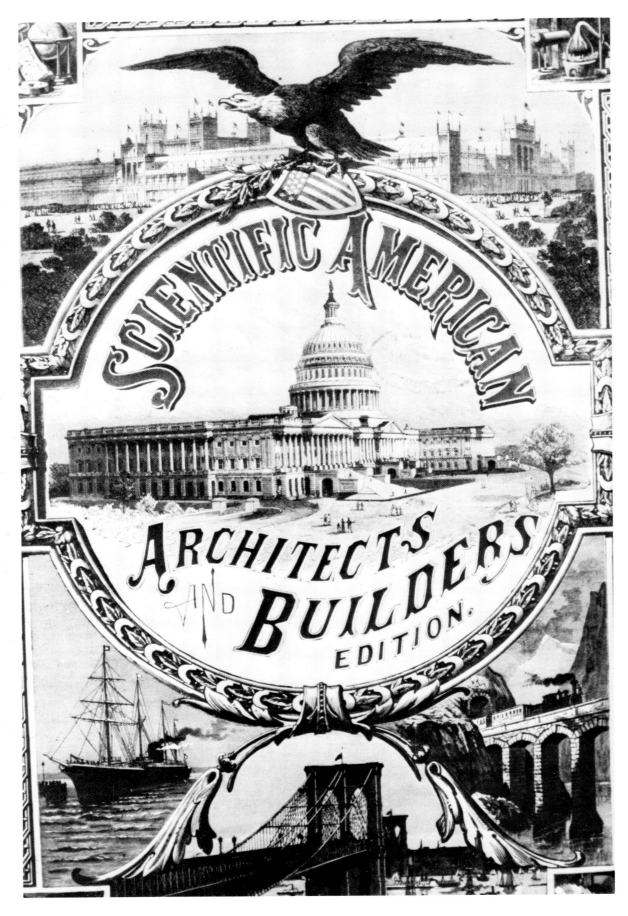

Illustration 3

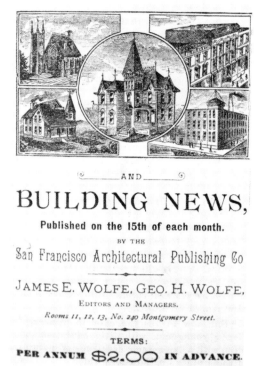

California Architect

AND

BUILDING NEWS,

Published on the 15th of each month.

BY THE

San Francisco Architectural Publishing Co

JAMES E. WOLFE, GEO. H. WOLFE,
EDITORS AND MANAGERS.

Rooms 11, 12, 13, No. 240 Montgomery Street.

TERMS:

PER ANNUM $2.00 IN ADVANCE.

Illustration 4

COMBINED STOOL AND BUSTLE.

Illustration 5

Plans & Patterns

From San Francisco to Washington, D.C., from Cape May to Little Rock, rows of tired townhouses have succumbed to an influx of commitment, new money, and fresh paint, in a colorful series of neighborhood revivals. A favorite target of the revivalists are Victorian homes, a vast collection in varied styles and materials, from the brownstones of Brooklyn to the redwood fantasies of the Pacific Coast, such as illustration 2.

The optimism of the late Nineteenth Century in the United States was best expressed in the variety and exuberance of its architecture. The Victorian wave of furious embellishment, which showcased the feverish fancy of the millwright's imagination, reached its crest as it crashed in San Francisco, washing the Pacific Coast with an infinity of structural enrichment. Many revivalists are seeking for the roots of this architecture, the origins of its shapes, styles, and adornments.

Two important influences on the Victorian builder are part of this text; their covers are illustrations 3 and 4. The eastern SCIENTIFIC AMERICAN builders' supplement and the CALIFORNIA ARCHITECT AND BUILDING NEWS provided monthly inspiration nationwide to thousands of architects, builders, and homebuyers. The inspirational message took a most practical turn in the form of house plans and specifications offered in each issue to provide subscribers with up-to-date and "tasty" ideas for home building.

Both magazines also provide humorous insights into the Victorian era, which was a time of contrasts. Inventors literally reached for the sky: One contrivance trapped large birds in a circular cage; as their wings flapped, it was supposed to rise gently to the clouds as a primitive version of the helicopter.[3] Yet fashion bound women firmly to the earth, in hourglass corsets and cumbersome petticoats, whose inconvenience was only slightly relieved by the device shown in illustration 5, which combined the decorative bustle with the practicality of a portable chair.

Mass Production

The 1876 Centennial Exposition in Philadelphia initiated America's "love affair with the machine" when six million people viewed fifty acres of exhibits. A new fancy for ornate house fronts, interiors, and furniture ensued, fed by a proliferation of machinery. Mass production of homes through balloon-framing and mass production of details combined with Victorian taste in lavish embellishment.[4] House plans and complete specifications were available everywhere; thus even the merchant builder could offer his customers decorated homes, and clerks, postmen, and policemen could live in Victorian rowhouses similar to architect-built extravaganzas.

Many of us now view mass production as dehumanizing, synonymous with shoddy workmanship and disposable products. Yet in the Nineteenth Century, the advantages of mass production allowed building on a wide scale, providing handsome homes even for lower-income families. These homes certainly were not carelessly constructed. In their second hundred years, many provide sound dwellings, and others are the target of willing revivalists awed by the durability of fragile-looking fancy-work.

Balloon-Framing

For centuries, homes were constructed in a complicated and time-consuming manner, more an exercise of cabinetry than carpentry. Large square timbers were anchored in the ground, then cross beams were carefully hand "tied," and all joints were thoroughly reinforced. This "mortice and tenon" method was tedious and required the concentrated work of several skilled craftsmen. Its product was a house frame which would literally stand by itself, without requiring the support of walls to hold it together.

A revolution in Nineteenth Century house-building was caused by the discovery that careful hand crafting was not necessary, because rows of thin studding could be quickly assembled with minimum crossbracing, and joints could be secured with machine-made wire nails. Then the siding, the horizontal boards which make up the skin of the house, could be nailed onto the studs, both holding the "balloon-frame" together and helping to support the roof members, as may be seen in illustration 6 found in the Appendix. A slight variant, "western platform framing," was developed in the western and southern United States soon after the introduction of balloon framing. A western framed building is constructed one story at a time, instead of all at once, and each floor becomes the "platform" for the construction of the next story. Using these framing methods, two men could construct a home quickly, and the skills required were measuring, sawing, and nailing, not careful joinery.[5]

This framing method originated in the midwest in 1839, when a builder realized that homes could be put up quickly if he took advantage of two new products, standardized lumber and machine-made nails. People scoffed at first; the name came from a critic who said the houses

Illustration 7

would blow away in a stiff breeze, like balloons.[6]

The durability of this method was even questioned during the 1880's by a San Francisco EVENING BULLETIN writer, who declared that a "common balloon-built redwood house" would be worn out and hard to rent in only ten years, thus impugning both the material and the manner of construction. Local architects responded quickly to this challenge to their craft. "Far-fetched and erroneous," they cried, asserting that the life of a house would not "be shortened by one tick of the clock because built 'balloon style'!"[7]

Once the house shell itself could be quickly built, the second component of Victorian building evolved, the many machines which made varieties of enrichment possible. The possibilities of combining balloon-framing and and mass-produced decorations were quickly exploited, as the architect encrusted his homes with enrichment drawn from the ages, while the merchant-builder produced blocks of "fancy" homes to sell to workers.

Early machines to produce decoration were simple gadgets powered by hand or foot; then horsepower, steam, gasoline, and electricity succeeded each other as the driving forces. From the jig-sawn lace of the sixties evolved the curved molding systems of the seventies, the explosion of wooden decorations of the eighties and the riotous plaster "rinceaux" of the nineties.

The machines were heavily promoted by the architectural magazines of the times, in elaborate advertisements showing bearded millwrights, such as illustrations 7 & 8, and in features describing the virtues of new items which just happened to be produced by advertisers. Prybil's fluting and twist machine was rated as the perfect device for the economical forming of "ornamental woodwork which the architect and home-builder now introduce so liberally on all handsomely finished structures."[8] Another machine from the same company was a combined corner block, rosette, dove tailing, and edge-molding machine designed to turn out "from 25 to 30 perfect corner blocks per minute."[9]

Where Did They Get Their Ideas?

The era of Victorian building produced embellished homes which marched from state to state to cover the nation with enough variety of shape, adornment, and price to satisfy any buyer. Aided by rapid construction methods and inexpensive mass-produced enrichments, certain home-building ideas caught fire. The results form a visual blaze of decorative details — peaked towers, lacy gables, pointed finials, hooded windows, and columned doorways.

Price, $15.00

IMPROVED No. 7 SCROLL SAW.

We warrant it to be well made, of good material and workmanship, and to saw Pine three inches thick at the rate of one foot per minute. Other woods in same proportion according to hardness.

Illustration 8

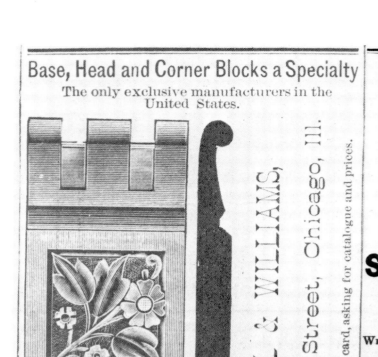
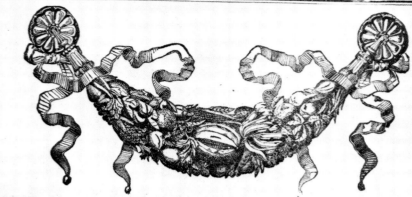

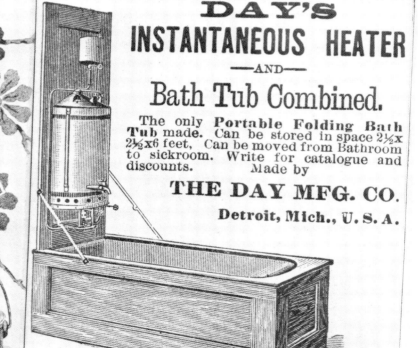
Illustration 9

A COTTAGE FOR FIFTEEN HUNDRED DOLLARS.

Illustration 10

A CALIFORNIA HOUSE FOR $2,500.

Illustration 11

PHILADELPHIA HOUSES OF MODERATE COST.

Illustration 12

Both individual architectural details and entire house plans recur across the country; sometimes patterns originated in stone are faithfully reproduced elsewhere in wood.

One way plans and patterns reverberated from coast to coast was through the circulation of books of elevations and specifications. Many thousands must have been available; some offered entire buildings, and others were volumes full of details, such as millwork, doors, or stair systems.

Too few have survived to trace their development fully, but fortunately another important source is practically complete, two widely-read monthly magazines written especially for architects and builders. The New York SCIENTIFIC AMERICAN ARCHITECTS AND BUILDERS EDITION (SA), which in 1887 gave itself credit for the largest circulation of any architectural or building paper in the world, crammed its pages with advice, advertisements such as illustration 9, and promotional features during its twenty years of publication from 1885 to 1905. Each issue contained at least two house plan elevations and complete specifications, as well as articles encouraging the use of new machinery with which rapid production of details was assured.

Its West Coast equivalent, the CALIFORNIA ARCHITECT AND BUILDING NEWS (CABN), was issued by the San Francisco Architectural Publishing Company. Its founding editor, James E. Wolfe, was born in Baltimore in 1821 and settled permanently in San Francisco in 1861, after a series of misadventures in mining and lumber. His son, George H., was both his partner in the architectural firm of Wolfe and Son and the joint manager and editor of the magazine.[10] The magazine was published from January, 1880 until July of 1900, although both Wolfes had long since relinquished control of it. After three years of publication, its circulation was reported as 52,000, and its goal as 100,000. The Wolfes established the magazine to counter erroneous opinions of California and the Pacific Coast and to supply principles to unify "diverse, diverging, and opposing views" of architecture in San Francisco.[11]

House Plans

The magazines offered many house plans during their decades of publication. A review of these features is a useful way to trace trends in design, public taste, and residential ornamentation. Both builders and their clients were concerned with costs: Illustrations 10, 11, and 12 show homes with low and moderate prices. Suburban residences were popular and ornate, as shown in illustrations 13 and 14. Nineteenth Century Americans often had country homes; four of varying design, size, and price are shown in illustrations 15 through 18. Numbers 15 & 16 are moderate in cost; 17 presents a "country store and flat," and 18 is a Victorian vision, heavily laden with ornament. In the provision of "city residences," illustrations 19 through 23, the two magazines were most prolific and most varied in cost, details, and sizes. Interior elements were featured, such as the balusters and newel posts in illustration 24. Ideas about interior decoration were also offered, as in 25, 26, and 27. By the turn of the century, the fittings were available for the handsomely-appointed bathroom shown in illustration 28, complete with bonzai tree and a slightly rumpled oriental rug.

The illustrations represent a striking diversity of style within a relatively short time span, a variety which the San Francisco magazine tried to describe as "from the 'old' and 'classic' orders modernized, down to strange conglomerations of individual conceptions of the beautiful." They felt that California was the particular target of this mixture because residents of the state had a "prevailing propensity" to experiment with new designs and forms, creating "irregularities and strange things."[12]

While the California magazine seemed embarrassed by the rowdy variety of San Francisco's Victorians, a New York architect celebrated the visual richness of his city. He enjoyed seeing all the best examples of foreign motifs, where Greek, Moorish, and Persian decorations might be the subject of "indiscriminate adaptation" and yet be pleasing even as next door neighbors:

> One is an excellent reproduction of a baronial castle on a small scale, with a moat, portcullis, watch tower, sentry box, and all. Still another is rambling . . . full of odd and queer corners, a marvelous quantity of stained glass, and a multitude of picturesque chimneys.[13]

A New York TIMES writer who visited San Francisco in 1883 also wrote in praise of architectural diversity:

> Nobody seems to think of building a sober house. Of all the efflorescent, floriated bulbousness, and flamboyant craziness that ever decorated a city, I think San Francisco may carry off the prize. And yet, such is the glittering and metallic brightness of the air, when it is not surcharged with fog, that I am not sure but this riotous run of architectural fancy is just what the city needs to redeem its otherwise hard nakedness.[14]

The magazine specifications, the house plan books,

Illustration 13

Illustration 14

Illustration 15

Illustration 16

Illustration 17

DESIGN FOR A COUNTRY SEAT.

Illustration 18

FRONT ELEVATION

Illustration 19

RESIDENCE OF C. H. LIGHT, CALIFORNIA STREET.—Plate 2

Illustration 20

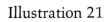

Illustration 21

Illustration 22

Illustration 23

Illustration 24

INTERIOR FITTED WITH SLIDING BLINDS AND SCREENS AND VENETIAN BLINDS.

Illustration 25

MOORISH DIVAN ON HALF STAIR LANDING.

Illustration 26

Illustration 28

BAY WINDOW DECORATIONS.

Illustration 27

and the detail catalogues made the variety possible, by providing both the carpenter-builder and the architect great stores of ideas and of actual "parts." Ideas in enrichment spread across the country; similar millwork items on similar houses can be seen in San Francisco, St. Louis, and New York, with variations due to local climate, materials, and geography. The magazines and their advertisements were an important influence in this cross-country pollination, providing inspiration to Victorians all over the United States. No wonder they used sources freely and combined with abandon!

How Did They Work?

Little is known about the work methods of the Victorian merchant builder, who often began as a carpenter and retired as a rowhouse contractor. New sources provide a glimpse into two lives, a carpenter-contractor of the 1860's, and a merchant-builder whose enormous legacy spanned almost a century.

George King Horton, illustration 29, was a young carpenter who came to San Francisco in 1858 with his wife, Maria, their high-back double bed, two dressers, and a shot gun. He was good at his craft, which he practiced for $21 a week in John Clark's shop on Sansome Street. Some faithfully transcribed excerpts from his 1864 diary, illustration 30, describe the life of a craftsman during that decade:

Illustration 29

Saturday, January 2, 1864: Shop closed. Went to Mr. MacLockim, got a pair of chickens.

Monday, January 4, 1864: This forenoon and part of afternoon making window frames . . . got to shop a little before quitting time and filed up my saw. The young hen laid her first egg today.

Tuesday, January 5, 1864: Went to work on Montgomery Street fitting up a bookstore . . . In the evening read *Frank Leslie's Lady's Magazine.*

Wednesday, January 6, 1864: At ten o'clock I went to the shop and commenced making six bath tubs.

Thursday, January 7, 1864: In shop all day making window frames this forenoon. This afternoon getting out finish. The hens laid two eggs today.

Friday, January 8, 1864: All three of the hens laid today for the first time.

Friday, January 15, 1864: I worked in the shop all

day capping pilasters for the 4th and Folsom Street house.

Friday, January 22, 1864: Maria has company, the two Miss Quicks. Anny Quick has had an offer of marriage, but Susy will not consent, so it stands for the present.

Sunday, January 31, 1864: All day we have had no company to molest us. I past the day reading the papers.

Friday, February 26, 1864: We had quite a heavy shock of an earthquake this morning about six o'clock. No damage done.

Friday, March 11, 1864: All alone today. I have been making window frames . . . We found our rooster dead under the nest.

Horton soon became a self-employed contractor who built many houses, including one noted in his diary for about $560 — $360 for materials and $200 for labor. Horton's longing to begin his own business may have caused these hints of impatience:

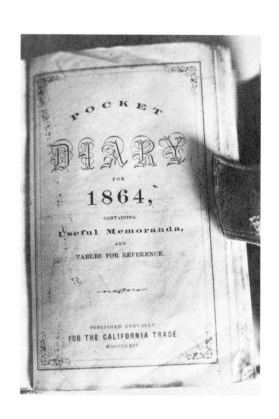

Illustration 30

Thursday, May 19, 1864: I went to Mr. Bryant's house on Third Street to finish up, but I had to leave to go to Mrs. Sweet's to do some jobbing.

Friday, May 20, 1864: I finished at Mrs. Sweet's at noon, I then went and finished Mr. Bryant on Third Street. Got done at three o'clock and went to the shop. Then I came home to do some work for myself.[15]

Fernando Nelson also began as a carpenter; he retired as San Francisco's most prolific builder, producing some 4,000 homes during the years he worked with his sons. His career spans almost a century, from the tiny flat-front Victorian he built at the age of sixteen to vast blocks in Park Merced Terrace.

During the 1880's and 1890's, Nelson built many rows of Victorian homes, which he sold for $1,000 to $4,500, depending on their size. These transactions were entered into a small receipt book which he carried in his hip pocket from 1876 until 1906. The book shows that his customers were usually clerks, policemen, firemen, and warehousemen, many of whom borrowed money from Nelson to complete their purchases.

For example, he lent $1,250 to Gustav Peck at 9 percent. Mr. Peck paid faithfully on the 15th of each month, and every payment was carefully inscribed in the receipt book by Nelson. Less than three years later, Mr. Nelson drew a large X across Peck's page, and wrote "paid in full and released" at the bottom. With M. C. Dunn, Nelson signed this contract in 1882: "April 3, agreed to build a 4-room cottage house on Alabama St., for $750." Mr. Dunn gave Nelson $100 in advance, with the balance in monthly payments of $20.

In May 1887, Nelson recorded specifications for the James Smith house on Brazil near Athens Street in the Outer Mission neighborhood:

sinks and doors	$130.00
lumber	350.00
tinning	6.50
painting	90.00
plumbing	50.00
plastering	140.00
centers (ceiling rosettes)	4.00
cresting	15.00
mantel	35.00
hardware	40.00
hauling	40.00
chimneys	37.00
labor	60.00
Total	$967.50

According to the receipt book, Nelson sold Smith the house for $1,330.50.

When Nelson began to build clusters of houses right next to each other, he used identical interior floor plans and outside embellishments. Home-buyers could make a few choices: A "plain" front door for $1.25, or a "fancy" one for $5.00; plaster or wallpaper inside. He sold a home on 4th Avenue to John and Louisa Stein, who wanted some extras: a golden oak mantel and light oak graining in the kitchen, bath, and small bedroom. They wanted their front door to be darker than one down the street, they ordered copper fixtures, and they instructed Nelson to paint the outside of the house "cream," like their neighbor's, but wanted the window sash "more green."

Nelson involved his entire family in his endeavors. His son George drove the rig, which was pulled by a horse named Bill. After Bill hauled lumber all day, he spent the evening walking a treadmill to power a saw to cut floor joists and studding for the next day's work. To save money, Nelson would buy broken kegs of nails down on the waterfront. On Sundays, Nelson would seat his family around the dining room table where they would sort out

1906 Columbia.

Illustration 31

nails by size. Nelson was an automobile buff who owned one of the first private cars in San Francisco. Illustration 31 shows fourteen-year-old George Nelson chauffering two officials and his father, the bearded man in the back seat. They were inspecting fire damage right after the 1906 earthquake.

Several "signature details" characterized his Victorian homes. Nelson's son says Fernando would "think up" these decorations and then have them produced "by the barrel" at the Townley Brothers Planing Mill on Berry Street between Third and Fourth Streets. Several Nelson signature details are intriguing because of his straightforward names for them. Over the entryway of some of his homes is a flat piece of wood jig-sawn into the shape of joined "O's". Nelson called them "donuts". He gave the name "drips" to a combination of halved dowels and balls which looked like dripping paint. "Bowties" were a simple ornament applied in the lower part of a square bay window, made from a piece of wood which resembled a baseball bat sawn in half.

Victorian builders usually constructed identical house shells with similar floor plans. The variation came from their choice and mixture of exterior embellishment. In San Francisco, builders were forced to design narrow rowhouses by the 25-foot wide parcels of land available; in other large cities, similar land constraints also resulted in closely spaced homes. In suburban areas or smaller towns, tracts were often built on larger lots, allowing the builder to produce a more expansive, more adorned home.

Most decorations came from local mills, where builders could thumb through the latest catalogue to choose among many kinds of doors, brackets, molding, and other trim, such as the entryways and windows in illustration 32, from the Niehaus Brothers Planing Mill in nearby West Berkeley. Some mills had "outside men" who traveled to the construction job sites to show millwork samples and take orders. Nelson sometimes ordered parts from the outside man from Townley's; other times he would take in his own designs, have them milled in great quantities, then "nail them onto the houses."

Like other merchant builders of the Victorian era, Nelson followed the street car and cable car lines and bought land as close to public transportation as possible. Nelson once said people should pay for a home according to its distance from the nearest car stop. After a certain distance, he felt, they should "be given the houses!" When he built some houses next to Golden Gate Park, he thought the park would be a good selling attraction. But the homes a block away sold first; "People were funny; they seemed to think the park was full of animals and undesirable people."[16]

618.

619.

PORTICOS

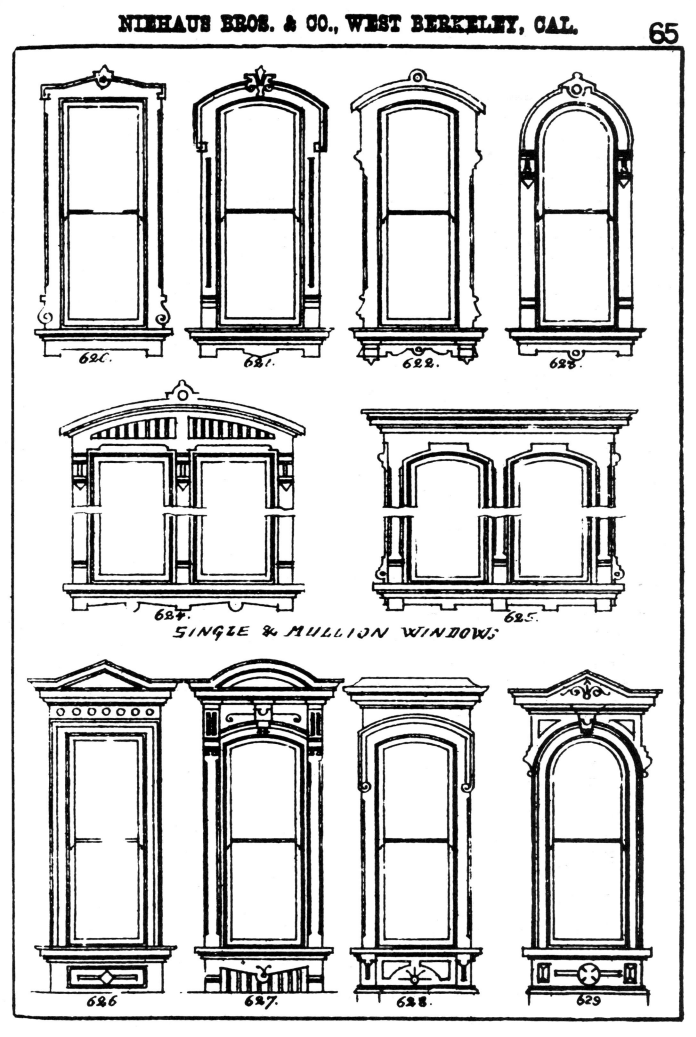

SINGLE & MULLION WINDOWS

Illustration 32

The legacy of Fernando Nelson and other carpenter-builders abounds in the previous photograph sections. Their work was admired in the Nineteenth Century, too, by this newspaper writer:

Not alone on Van Ness Avenue and California Street, so long honored as the 'show' streets of San Francisco, but far out on Haight and Valencia, along the remotest cross streets of the Western Addition sprang, thick and fast, the most elegant residences that wealth and taste could produce. All along the lines of the great cable roads, there was excavating and nailing and hammering, and the rearing of beautiful homes where a few years before had been a wilderness of sand and sagebrush.[17]

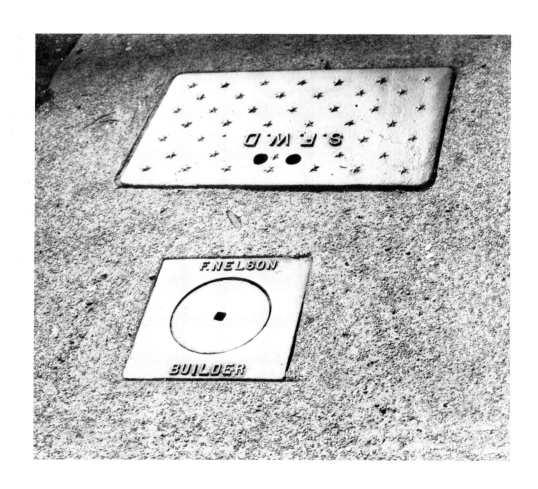

What About Styles?

Fernando Nelson and his building crews used to construct the basic house and then "put on a front." They didn't refer to them by style name, but as "3, 4, 5 room houses," or as "stud houses," because of the studding used to frame them. This lack of standard names was described during the era:

> For a long time, the public mind seemed powerless to conceive of anything more sublime than the conventional bay-windowed house . . . Just when the present esthetic movement began, it would be hard to determine; but it first manifested itself in a growing aversion to gray paint. Cautiously at first, and then more and more boldly, houses appeared in browns, yellows, greens, and even reds — all sorts of unorthodox colors; yet one was forced to admit that the town did look better for it. To this end followed a series of extravagant creations in which oddity was the prevailing characteristic. There were houses with no two sides or windows alike, houses of chaste and rigid outline and houses all angles and florid garniture; houses as eccentric and scrappy as a crazy quilt, apparently pieced together from the leavings of other houses.[18]

A close examination of plans, both those in books and those published in architectural magazines, reveals that style "names" were seldom attached to individual houses. As shown in the previous sample of house plans, illustrations 2 and 10 through 23, price or location were the descriptive words most frequently used.

Tract builders today vary their house facades. Under the trappings of fluttering flags and spot lights, buyers may find the "Spanish," the "Colonial," the "Riviera," or the "Western Ranchette." So did the builders of the Nineteenth Century try to tempt the imaginations of the home-buying public. Some of the descriptions went beyond place or price, such as "modern," "tasty," or "picturesque." Some loosely defined style names were used, as shown in 33, 34, and 35, which are plan book advertisements. But the homes they described seldom had any common shapes or details, and a "semi-colonial" one month might become "An American Renaissance dwelling" the next.

That the earlier designers of house plans seldom gave style names to their work is further substantiated by A. J. Bicknell's 1878 volume, SPECIMEN BOOK OF ONE HUNDRED ARCHITECTURAL DESIGNS. Aimed at two audiences, "those who wish a home, and those who build for the purposes

Illustration 33

Illustration 34

Illustration 35

of investment," Bicknell compiled one hundred samples representing that many different catalogues and pattern books. Forty-one of those designs were house plans, and the rest are architectural details, churches, stables, mantels, and a bank front. Not one of the house plans was assigned a style name. As in the two magazines, some names were functional, "cheap country cottages," "a parsonage house," and others were descriptive: "a French-roofed house," "a half-timbered cottage," "a commodious English cottage."[19]

The word "Victorian" is loosely applied to the whole conglomeration; to many even the application of the name of a British sovereign to United States buildings is puzzling. But until the early Twentieth Century, we always used the name of a British monarch to characterize style and taste during his or her reign: "Tudor," "Elizabethan" and "Edwardian" are prominent examples. To name our exuberant homes after Victoria seems particularly fitting, since her reign of two-thirds of a century was described as one of great progress "affecting all classes in their domestic life and prosperity."[20]

Style names are important as a shorthand way to describe buildings and as a map to follow the trail of different influences. But a "style" must have certain attributes, including consistency of basic shape and standard pattern of details. To trace these paths among the bewildering variety of Victorians is difficult. Two such paths are those which led to the "Eastlake" and to the "Queen Anne" styles. "Eastlake" was repudiated as a house style, both by the man himself and by architects of the era, but Queen Anne survived initial ridicule and wavering to become the home which to many symbolizes the frivolous fancy of the entire Victorian era.

The Eastlake Craze

From the roots of the 1876 Philadelphia Centennial Exposition grew a fad which for a time inundated the country. Charles Locke Eastlake, whose furniture was featured there, was a British interior decorator whose oft reprinted book HINTS ON HOUSEHOLD TASTE became the unwitting

Illustration 36

justification for house plans and furniture. Then "Eastlake" degenerated into meaningless and widespread popularity. For example, the SCIENTIFIC AMERICAN specified in one of its plans "an 18 x 30 Mott's Eastlake galvanized iron sink," and the Joost Brothers, San Francisco hardware importers, advertised "a complete assortment of locks, including the Eastlake design." The Eastlake name was also attached to doors, mantels, paint and even a brand of shingles, as shown in illustration 36.[21]

An important question to explore, from the dispassionate distance of some ninety years, is the correspondence between the "Eastlake" plans and products and the principles of design and decoration extolled in HINTS ON HOUSEHOLD TASTE. Even a cursory review of the book reveals the truth of Eastlake's plaintive request to stop attaching his name to items he found "extravagant and bizarre." In his book Eastlake sets forth commandments of taste and design: his wish for decorative treatment in an "honest and straightforward manner"; his characterization of machine-made "scrollwork" as "trash"; his calling a good design "not only picturesque but practical and workmanlike." He felt the decorator should "*typify*, not represent, the works of Nature . . . nor are the fairest flowers which bloom suitable objects to be copied literally for surface ornament." He favored incised decorations which were "chaste and sober in design, never running into extravagant contour or unnecessary curves."[22]

Since this book is about Victorian homes, a review of "Eastlake" house plans will be useful to answer two questions. First, have they the consistency of form, pattern, and detail which are essential for a group of buildings to be labeled as all examples of the same "style", regardless of name? Second, do the plans indeed "burlesque" the ideas of the man?

At least eight plans for "Eastlake" houses were published between 1880 and 1887, but these plans had few common features and quite dissimilar shapes. Five are illustrated here and discussed below; the sixth was published by the New York architectural firm of William Comstock.[23] His 1881 book, MODERN ARCHITECTURAL DESIGNS AND DETAILS, had plans for more than forty houses and elevations of hundreds of details. The word "Eastlake" was used only once, to describe a broad brick residence with two tall decorative chimneys and several gables topped by finials. With a minor bit of imagination applied, the house could be a brick version of an "Eastlake" organ exhibited by the Mason and Hamlin Company at the Philadelphia Centennial. The organ has a major triangular centerpiece, much like the main gable of the house elevation, and both were topped with a finial.[24]

The same year six "Eastlake Style" plans were

published in San Francisco. Illustrations 37 and 38 were prepared by the Newsom Brothers, San Francisco architects later famed for designing the massive Carson House in Eureka, California. Their "Eastlake Cottages" were much less ornate than the New York Comstock version, having in common roofline cresting, several finials, and a gable ornament composed of several turned pieces of wood joined together to resemble a brace. Both had rectangular floors plans, no bays, and peaked roofs, but one had a square tower on the back end.[25] In that same issue, the magazine presented yet another version of the "Eastlake Style". Illustration 39 shows a two-story, slanted bay-windowed home whose main similarity to the other two was its braced gable and its roofline cresting and finials — the decorative wood or ironwork used in virtually every plan then being published in San Francisco.[26]

Two months later, another "cottage in the Eastlake Style" was featured with a two story veranda on one side, both square and polygonal bays, and half-timber ornaments. Illustration 40 shows its roof was steeply sloped, topped with the usual cresting, finials, and dormer windows. Its major feature was a squared semi-tower with a pyramid roofline.[27]

The SCIENTIFIC AMERICAN paid little heed to the Eastlake fad, beyond printing advertisements and promotional features for various "Eastlake" products. Only one house plan appeared, illustration 41, and its source was given as a California architect, David Salfield. The comment was sparing; aside from specifying such items as "a Golden Gate water closet," it reported, "The elevation is of the Eastlake style and needs very little description." The house has a central recessed entryway, twin squared bays with "braced" gables, and a row of iron cresting punctuated by a finial at either end.[28]

The "Eastlake" homes which originated in California have virtually no resemblance to the large brick Eastern dwelling with "features" published by Comstock. But their resemblance to each other is also faint, unless a style definition can be based on decorative ironwork, which was common to most homes at that time, or on a single detail, the braced gable.

Keep Eastlake's decorative principles in mind as you examine the "Eastlake" house plans. If he favored "chaste and sober" designs, none of these embellished confections would qualify, with their extraneous, though decorative, roofline cresting and finials. The only possible connections might be two: An Eastlake table design has a device which might be transformed into a braced gable. Eastlake's preference for incised ornament might be construed as a reason for grafting his name to certain features on the exteriors of some Victorian homes. Yet, incised and jig-sawn orna-

Illustration 37

Illustration 38

Illustration 39

Illustration 40

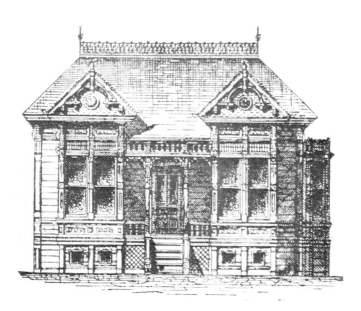

Illustration 41

ments were common as window decorations in San Francisco in the 1870's, well before the Philadelphia Exposition. Incised wooden enrichment became even more important during the 1880's, a trend which owed more to available machinery than to Eastlake's influence reaching westward.

The CALIFORNIA ARCHITECT AND BUILDING NEWS conducted a lengthy battle against the "Eastlake" houses. They chastised any architect who adopted the term, because they found it:

> not a classic order of architecture with defined principles of treatment and rules of application and delineation . . . So unrestrained in its requirements that the wildest conceits of the mediocre pretender may be imposed and the most absurd and distinctive features defined as in keeping with the style . . . Its excessive gaudery would cause rejection as a 'style,' except by a limited number who prefer oddities . . . Could Eastlake behold some of the extra delineations, he would doubtless cry to the gods to blot out the monstrosities.[29]

The editors soon prevailed upon the man to cry out, if not to the gods, at least to their subscribers. They mailed him the editorial and some designs of "so-called Eastlake houses" and asked for his opinion. Eastlake's reply was both a disavowal and an indictment of the application of his name to either houses or furniture. He first stated that his views were entirely in accord with the editorial, then continued,

> For some years past, it has been my fate to see illustrated and hear of objects manufactured in America under the name of 'Eastlake' furniture which I not only never designed, but which represented a taste very far removed from and often directly opposed to the principles of art and workmanship I have endeavored to advocate. That I cannot be held responsible . . . may be inferred from the fact that not a single American manufacturer . . . has thought it worthwhile to consult me.

Thus disposing of the furniture given his name, he soundly renounced the "Eastlake Style" of architecture:

> I now find, to my amazement, that there exists . . . an 'Eastlake' style of architecture, which, judging from the specimens I have seen illustrated may be said to burlesque such doctrines of art as I have ventured to maintain . . . I feel greatly flattered by the popularity which my books have attained in

America, but I regret that their author's name should be associated there with a phase of taste in architecture and industrial arts with which I can have no real sympathy and which by all accounts seems to be extravagant and *bizarre*. (Signed) Your obedient servant, Charles Locke Eastlake.[30]

Mere wishing on the part of the editors did not halt the "Eastlake" fad, so they retaliated by berating builders whose decorations were "accomplished by a liberal plastering on of 'gingerbread' work." They even attacked the colors used on "Eastlake" houses:

hoods over windows of a chocolate color, relieved by brackets and painted with a beautiful *coleur de mouse* (sic), window sash of red . . . , the upper sash of the windows divided into small squares, so that in case of necessity they can be taken out and used for checkerboards; a few dozen strips of wood, beautifully interlaced for a cornice, giving the birds a nice roosting place for their weary feet.[31]

By September, 1886, the California magazine felt its campaign had succeeded, and it published illustration 42, a "Representative San Francisco Dwelling", which was "the average architecture of . . . those who move in the well-to-do walks of life." It felt the exterior was "in perfectly good taste, without any attempt to clap on the *balderdashian* styles commonly but erroneously styled as Eastlake . . ."[32]

A REPRESENTATIVE SAN FRANCISCO DWELLING.

Illustration 42

Queen Anne

The Queen Anne fancy also had its roots in the Philadelphia Centennial Exposition, where the British exhibit's decorative chimneys, steep ornamented gables, and layers of stone and brick would eventually be embraced by America's builders and desired by its home-buying public. The same glut of criticism accompanied this departure from tradition as that aroused by "Eastlake", but Queen Anne evolved as a definite style and survived a period of severe ridicule. Since the Queen was a deceased monarch, no meddling magazine could write for her opinion of the style and use her views to castigate those builders who succumbed to the seductive sound of a "modern" name in house plans. As a result, the carpings were dissipated by time, and by the turn of the century the archetypes of the Queen Anne style were solidly established and generally accepted.

In California, the CABN editors first found these faults with the style, although they later favored it:

facades loaded with inappropriate and meretricious ornamentation, like an overdressed vulgar woman . . . Our habits and ways of living are so like those of the people of Europe that we have adopted their styles, and we show here every feature of the different houses of the old country mixed up together.

Of all the absurdities of modern house-building, this attempt to push in the Queen Anne style of 1700 is the worst . . . The Queen Anne houses will become a drug in the market, and they will depreciate the property on which they are located.[33]

The basic elements of form and decoration which now comprise the Queen Anne style were given a whole series of other names in the plans and house descriptions promoted in magazine features. The shape that springs instantly to the mind of contemporary Americans is the turreted home, punctuated by some form of tower. Yet the tower device appeared in the San Francisco magazine first in 1883, where it was merely another decoration added to a "suburban residence," illustration 13, not an essential element of its style. In the Eastern magazine, a "tower house," illustration 48, did not appear until 1890, topping a home which it labeled "a mixture of Queen Anne and Colonial." The next year another "tower house" plan was presented, illustration 23, without assigning any style name. Then a few months later the magazine offered a "Queen Anne cottage," which it billed as "a very rare and tasty bit of Rural Architecture." Yet this house resembled neither the loosely-held definition of Queen Anne in the 1890's nor the assemblage of parts now assigned that name.[34]

Early in 1892, the SCIENTIFIC AMERICAN first pictured the "American Renaissance Style of Architecture,"[35] which would now be classified as Queen Anne, and, second, a belvedered and gabled house with spindlework and three stained glass windows. This second home they called "designed in the style of modern Romanesque."[36] By the mid 1890's, the style had coalesced, but its title still varied. Thus one month, this "Modern Dwelling in Connecticut" shown in illustration 43, was offered: "The design shows good features, including a broad piazza, pleasant balcony and a tower, which adds dignity." Another month, virtually the same elevation was described as "American Architecture."[37] The final variant was called the "English Gothic style, with a suggestion of Romanesque: an octagonal tower, broad treatment of gables and bays, richness of detail of frieze, bands, and bargeboards."[38]

That description typifies what in San Francisco came to be known as a "Queen Anne," in two shapes, the "tower house" and the steep-gabled "rowhouse." Those style

Illustration 43

names were not applied originally in California either, but before the first Queen Anne plan appeared, the western magazine reported on a trend which was associated with the new style, a radical change in floor plan arrangements.

San Francisco house lots were commonly 25 feet wide, a factor taken into account in most plans presented in the magazine. To conform to this size, most homes of the 1860's through the early 1880's had identical plans, with a long narrow hallway and many doors. But in 1883, it announced a new fashion and described a change in room arrangements which came to typify the Queen Anne interior: "One of the most pleasant and attractive of the later fashions is that of arranging the plan of a house so the entrance 'hall' shall be something more than a long, narrow passage into which the stairs obtrusively crowd." It felt such a hall would become "the very center and heart of the home, an improvement over the straight-and-narrow, formal halls that belong to old-fashioned houses."[39]

Not until more than a year later was such a plan published. The editors proposed a house plan contest and invited entries nationwide. Their four winners were Eastern architects; each "premium" house contained Queen Anne features, although they were not called such by the magazine. The contest seemed to mark the initial appearance of a "tower house" in California. In describing illustration 44, they reported, "The house is certainly picturesque in its outside appearance. We have not seen anything resembling it in this state." The elevation, with its horizontal demeanor, its tower, its gabled roof, and its plaster adornment, differed totally from the usual magazine plan for a vertical, rectangular home laden with wooden decoration.[40]

Thus was ushered into California the Queen Anne house, although it was not so named until later. Though faint critical rumblings were heard at the turn of the century about "the terrible tower or the equally terrible turret," the towered Queen Anne has become one of the most beloved and dramatic symbols of the Victorian era.[41] The California magazine even featured illustration 45, in which a home was completely transformed by grafting on a towered addition. While both magazines correctly identified "Eastlake" as a quicksilver fad which soon faded, they initially misjudged Queen Anne, whose captivating fancy still prevails, an eloquent example of the craft of the Victorian builder.

FRONT ELEVATION OF $5,000 COUNTRY DWELLING.—SECOND PREMIUM DESIGN.

Illustration 44

RESIDENCE OF JOHN L. BOONE

Illustration 45

Pelton's Cheap Dwellings

Competition between the Victorian architect and the merchant builder became overt when a San Franciscan published a series of copyrighted low-cost house plans in a daily newspaper. The SCIENTIFIC AMERICAN observed the same kind of competition in the East, which was characterized as the sale of "ready-made misfit building plans." These plans enabled builders and owners to dispense with the services of an architect altogether and to produce the "repetitive rowhouse" which the editors felt "disfigured so many neighborhoods."[42]

The San Francisco series was commissioned by the EVENING BULLETIN, because its editors perceived a new trend in home building: "Street railroads are reaching out to the suburbs, making available the unimproved outside lands which can be bought at prices within the reach of all persons." To help these people build homes, the newspaper decided to publish its own plans for them to use. This gesture, it explained, was caused by the refusal of local architects to design a low-cost home, "on the grounds that the compensation was insufficient." The series was prepared by John Pelton, Jr., a local architect who described his "Cheap Dwellings" as "trustworthy and economic plans for small families of moderate means."

During the Victorian era, "cheap" simply meant low in cost, without the implications of inferior material or poor workmanship the word carries today. Pelton's basic house plan specified the same materials and used the same framing method as other homes built at the time. He achieved economy by making the homes small in size, by sacrificing some exterior elaborations, and by calling for an extremely plain interior finish.

Pelton gave these cost estimates for Dwelling No. 1, a three-room house:

286

287

288

excavations, cesspits & drainpipes	10.00
lumber, 3800 ft.	68.00
flooring, 570 ft.	15.00
Rustic (siding), 1800 ft.	50.00
shingles, $8^{1}/_{2}$ m.	17.00
doors, windows & millwork	40.00
carpenter, labor & nails	130.00
chimney	115.00
mantel	20.00
plastering	55.00
painting	45.00
plumbing & tinwork	20.00
Total	$585.00[43]

The initial magazine reaction was mild; perhaps the editors thought the "series" would fade quietly without progeny, because they contented themselves with criticizing the low estimates and the lack of a railing on the outside stairway.[44] But Pelton persisted and produced No. 2, "very neat and handsome", priced at $854.25.[45] The Wolfes quickly replied, "No. 2 is handsome to those who consider it so, but . . . cannot be erected in any sort of *workmanlike & substantial manner* for the sum named."[46]

289

Plans 1 and 2 were straightforward, relatively unadorned small buildings, but No. 3 was more ornate and cost $1,140. The magazine retorted: "Well, there is no accounting for taste. There is possibly someone who can admire the ugly thing . . . We doubt the necessity of copyrighting the access to living room and kitchen . . . There is not the least danger that any competent architect will copy anything so far produced."[47]

Pelton and the BULLETIN continued the series, seemingly oblivious to the apoplectic editorials, which next called the plans "delusive in character and merit" and likely to "create erroneous impressions and corrupt the minds of property owners, particularly those of limited means."[48]

The magazine summed up "the Peltonian era in Architecture" by judging the man "a peculiar personage" who has made himself "conspicuous by peculiar, irregular, extraordinary, and visionary acts." They cast aside his plans as "delusive, inaccurate, and untrue," also as "defective, insufficient and grossly incorrect."[49]

290

Both Pelton and the BULLETIN emerged unscathed; in 1883, another series of "copyrighted Cheap Dwellings" was introduced. The newspaper was proud of the results of its efforts: "It is apparent The Series has been instrumental in introducing and popularizing a new style of architecture in San Francisco, as evidenced by the form of many of the dwellings which have been erected in the past two years."[50] The magazine responded: "It is little better than an insult to the architects of San Francisco to assert that a single one . . . has derived a single thought from the Bulletin."[51]

It is impossible to trace accurately the effect of Pelton's "Cheap Dwellings" on Nineteenth Century San Francisco. Many owners may have taken his plans directly from the newspaper and made their own additions or subtractions, and merchant builders probably adopted his plans to their rowhouse customers. The criticisms of local architects were obviously not heeded by home buyers of the time, because as these photographs show, the influence of Pelton was abiding.

291

"What Is Past Is Prologue"

292

293

294

These words from Shakespeare's *Tempest* are at the root of the Victorian revival movement, as across the nation our heritage of robustly decorated buildings is being reclaimed as prologue to a new future. A strong revival spur is a quickened awareness of how much of our architectural heritage has vanished, not into the cold storage of stucco to await eventual resurrection, but lost forever to redevelopment, replacement, or wanton plunder by salvage companies who found the houses worth more dismembered.

Contemporary revivalists hurry to save Victorians, lest we are forced to echo this 1897 lament for the loss of virtually all colonial buildings in New York City:

> every few years we make another sacrifice of old buildings to the gods of economy, space and acquirement of wealth, and it is strange there would be any examples still remaining.[52]

The Victorian reclamation is imbued with concern for the true meaning of restoration: reverence for the original vision of the builder or architect. The complex millwork which makes Victorians such a pleasure to view can make them a puzzle to restore. Solving the puzzle used to mandate use of wrecking ball plunder, as the leavings of demolition crews became the foundation for a redone facade, too rarely applied with sensitivity to scale or concern for the original plans of the builder. But with the advent of authentic restoration specialists, complete facade reconstruction is a reality, and even the non-handyman can rescue a Victorian, foregoing the endless search through salvage yards.

Misguided Improvements

The photograph section of *A Gift to the Street* shows both architect-designed and merchant-built homes. However, it does not catalogue an important segment of the builders' archives, the "misguided improvements" now the target of revivalists. These homes have been disguised by alterations, grim reminders of a time when people found Victorians embarrassing in their decorative exuberance. The joyous excess spawned by the Victorian builder has always been a target. At an architects' convention in 1900, one speaker said, "inordinate accumulations of wealth by people who lack corresponding degrees of culture may result in the vulgar and ostentatious overadornment of their buildings."[53]

Soon after that condescending judgment, the first ammunition appeared in the battle against the "vulgar and ostentatious." In July, 1901, asbestos shingles were heralded as "very thin, hard and homogeneous, can be cut and nailed like a board, practically indestructible."[54] Asbestos was the vanguard weapon, as whole blocks of embellished homes were shorn of detail and disguised by products of the Johns-Manville Company, as illustrated in photograph 295.[55]

Later misguided improvements proved even more influential: Stucco salesmen showed how a Victorian rowhouse could masquerade as a Spanish villa, complete with red tile roof. Photograph 296 shows a Victorian with amputated bay windows, sullied with stucco. Permastone procurers tempted owners by promising to make a rowhouse into a medieval fortress, such as photograph 297.

While some offending modernizations were promoted as making an old house more fashionable, economy was an equally important factor. Aluminum siding was touted by a shapely model hosing off dirt, instead of repainting. The newest way to save money is by spraying on a coating textured like flacid chewing gum mixed with hair, virtually impossible to remove without destroying wooden or plaster detail.

An awareness of the extent of misguided improvements is a crucial revival element: A recent survey of eight San Francisco neighborhoods found half of 13,487 Victorian buildings disguised as something else, a discovery which doubles the potential reservoir for restoration.[56]

With so many denuded Victorians to be reclothed, reconstruction is being approached in different ways. Some revivalists feel that removing the asbestos or stucco is the most urgent task and that any combination of wooden details is appropriate as a substitute for the misguided improvement. Yet these house fronts are our legacy of Nineteenth Century American architecture and as such belong to all of us. Their restoration must be approached with reverence for the original plan of the architect or builder.

This level of authenticity is the aim of the best of the new restoration craftsworkers, who are an essential element of the Victorian revival. For example, the restoration specialists at San Francisco Victoriana have compiled the old pattern books and have found the millworking machinery necessary to design and produce entire house fronts which are authentic recreations of the original buildings.

A Gift to the Street is a journey through one place, contemporary San Francisco. We focused on a single city to show the breadth of its Victorian resources, both potential revivals and realized ones, and to suggest the varieties of homes which graced cities all over America at the turn

295

296

297

of the century. The photographs show modest homes and grand ones; we present them as an invitation to search for the Victorians in your own neighborhood or city. Go outside; see the buildings in their surroundings, amidst the automobiles, dogs and people who also use the street.

Learning to look is a pleasure; the buildings will embrace your eyes. Look underneath the disguises; imagine the original house constructed by the builder. Find in the homes which are still intact reminders of the plans and patterns which inspired them, such as the examples shown in illustrations 46 through 48. Enjoy the legacy of the anonymous Victorian builder, who may have offered his gift to our streets in this spirit:

> *Creating, yet not possessing,*
> *working, yet not taking credit,*
> *the work is done, then forgotten.*
> *Therefore it lasts forever.*

Illustration 46

298

299

Illustration 47

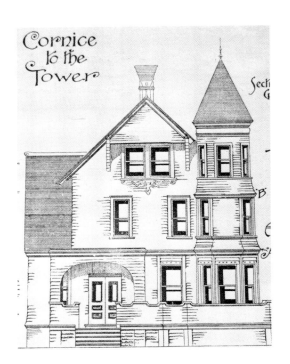

Illustration 48

300

APPENDIX

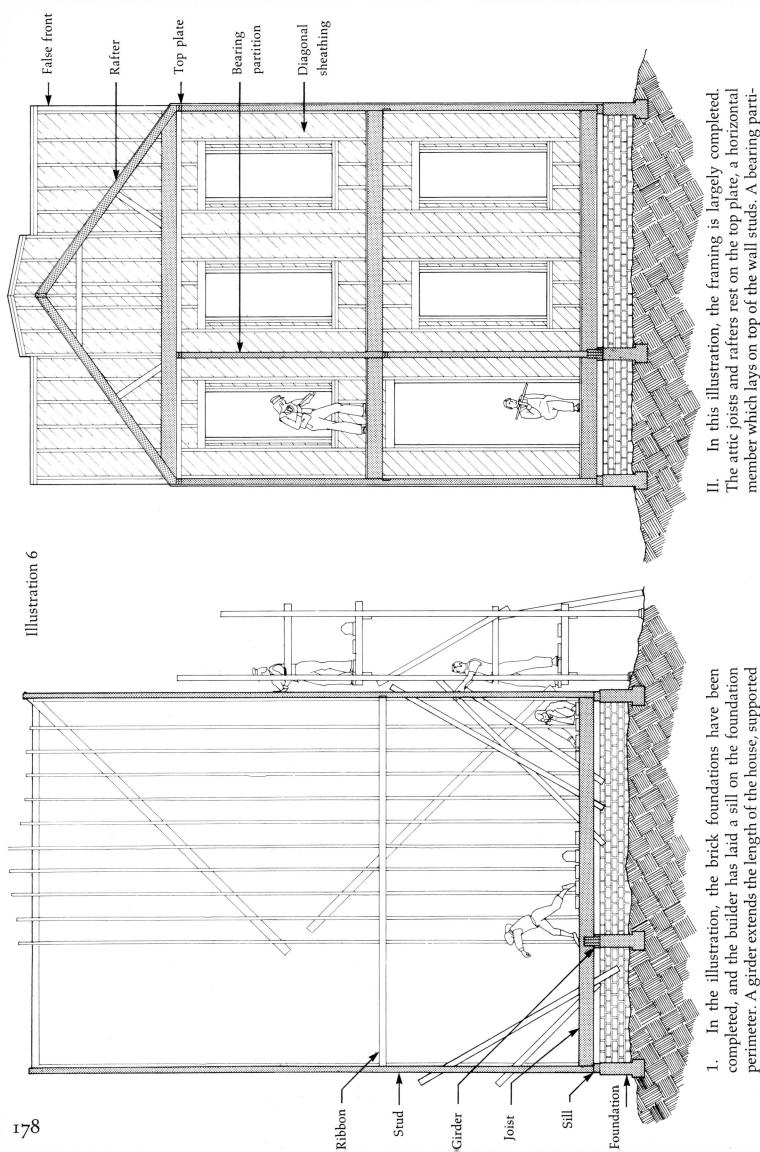

Illustration 6

False front
Rafter
Top plate
Bearing partition
Diagonal sheathing

Ribbon
Stud
Girder
Joist
Sill
Foundation

II.   In this illustration, the framing is largely completed. The attic joists and rafters rest on the top plate, a horizontal member which lays on top of the wall studs. A bearing partition extends from the girder below to the underside of the second story and attic joists, providing additional support for the floors. A false front is formed by continuing the front wall framing to the desired height. The carpenters have framed the window and door openings, and have nailed diagonal sheath-ing to the outside, lending rigidity to the frame.

1.   In the illustration, the brick foundations have been completed, and the builder has laid a sill on the foundation perimeter. A girder extends the length of the house, supported by brick or wooden piers, and floor joists span the intervals between the sills and girder. The carpenters have erected a scaffold and are busy placing the vertical corner posts and studs which frame the outside walls. These they secure by means of temporary braces. A horizontal ribbon ties the studs to the outside, lending rigidity to the frame, and provide support for the second story floor joists.

178

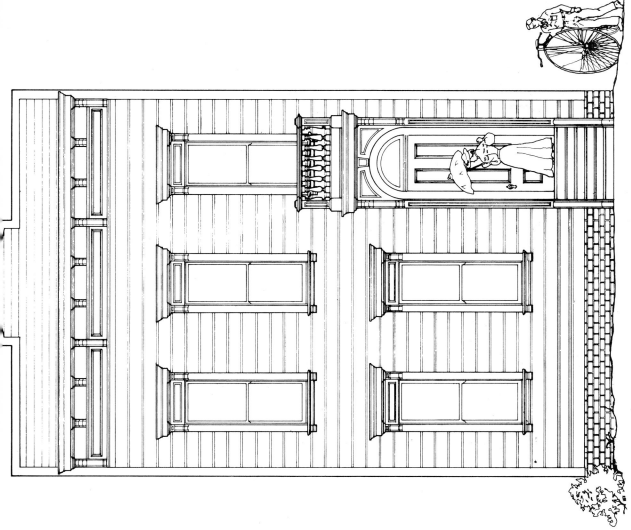

IV.   The newly completed residence.

Balloon Frame Construction

Drawings by Stephen Rynerson, architectural designer,
San Francisco Victoriana.

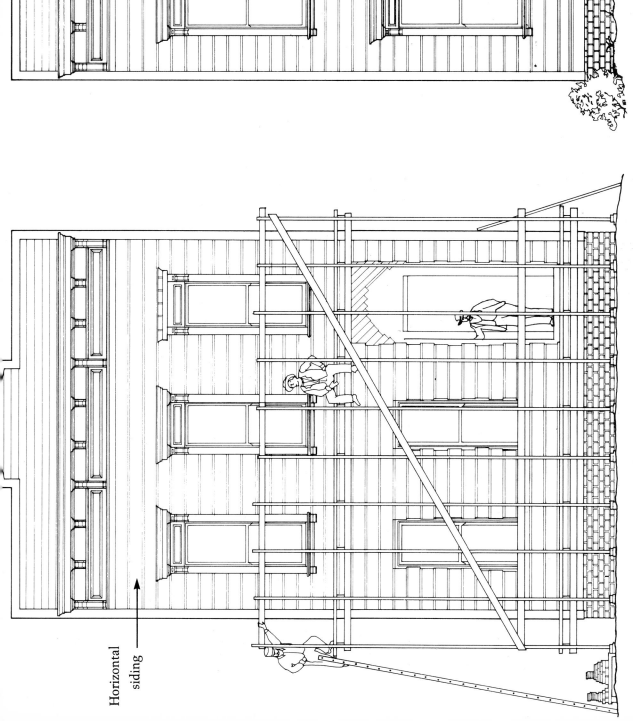
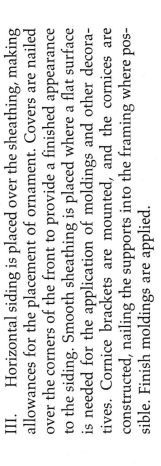

Horizontal
siding

III.   Horizontal siding is placed over the sheathing, making allowances for the placement of ornament. Covers are nailed over the corners of the front to provide a finished appearance to the siding. Smooth sheathing is placed where a flat surface is needed for the application of moldings and other decoratives. Cornice brackets are mounted, and the cornices are constructed, nailing the supports into the framing where possible. Finish moldings are applied.

Flat Front Italianate

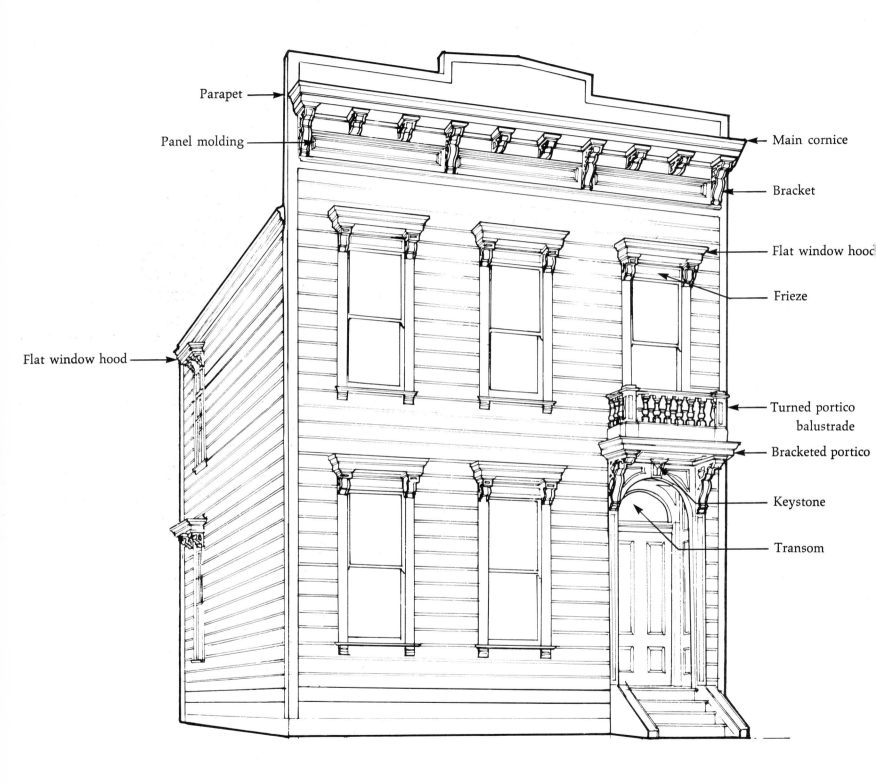

Parapet

Panel molding

Flat window hood

Main cornice

Bracket

Flat window hood

Frieze

Turned portico balustrade

Bracketed portico

Keystone

Transom

Italianate With Slanted Bay

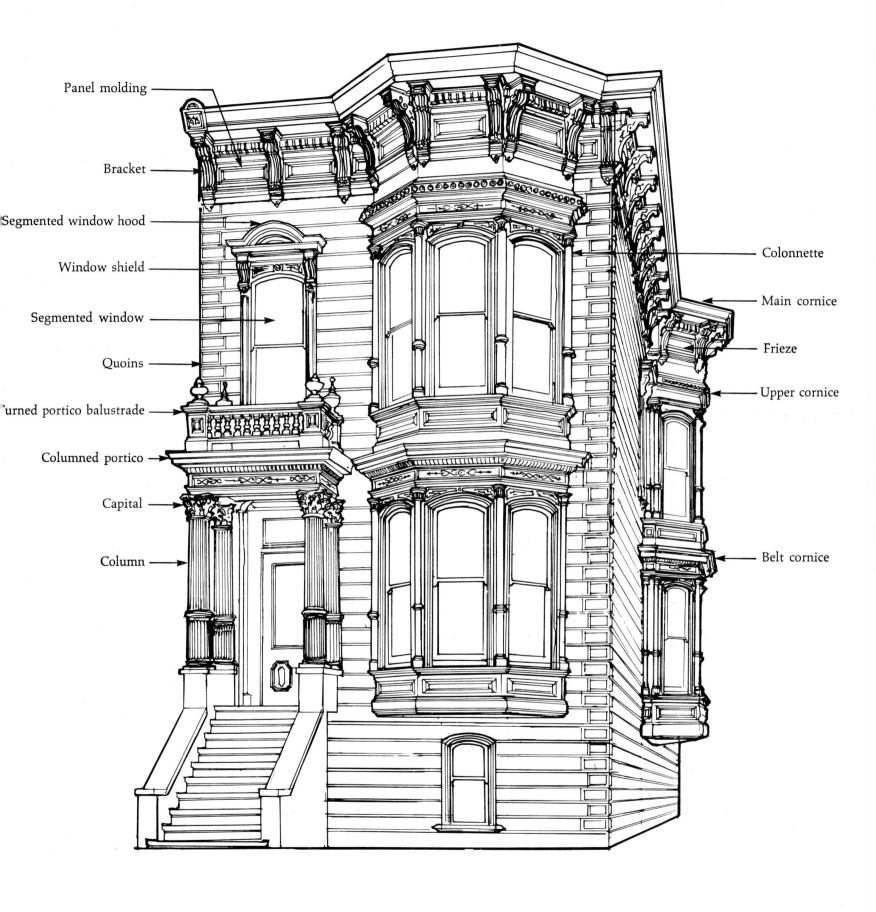

Panel molding

Bracket

Segmented window hood

Window shield

Segmented window

Quoins

Turned portico balustrade

Columned portico

Capital

Column

Colonnette

Main cornice

Frieze

Upper cornice

Belt cornice

Queen Anne Tower House

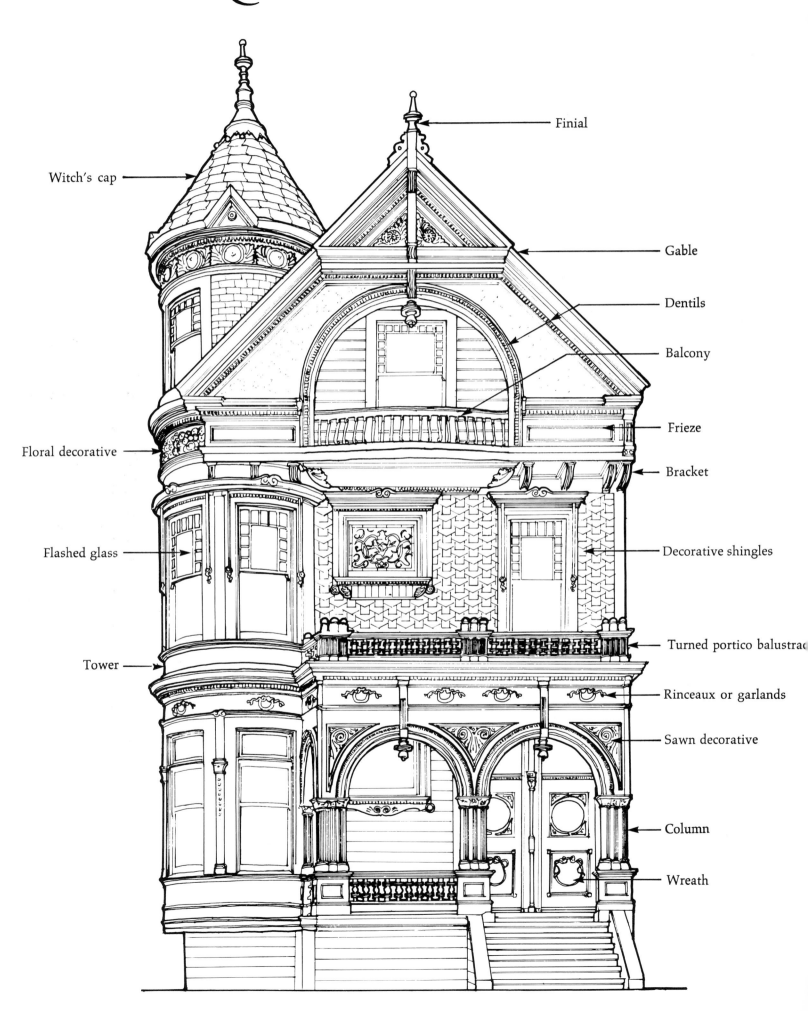

Witch's cap

Finial

Gable

Dentils

Balcony

Frieze

Floral decorative

Bracket

Flashed glass

Decorative shingles

Turned portico balustrad

Tower

Rinceaux or garlands

Sawn decorative

Column

Wreath

San Francisco Stick

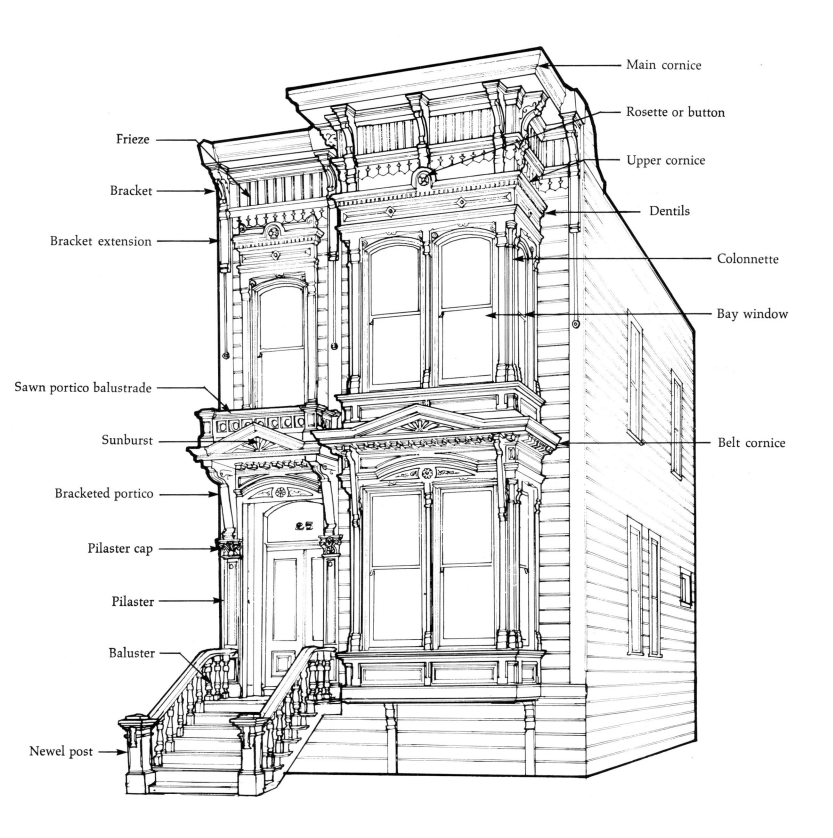

Main cornice

Rosette or button

Frieze

Upper cornice

Bracket

Dentils

Bracket extension

Colonnette

Bay window

Sawn portico balustrade

Sunburst

Belt cornice

Bracketed portico

Pilaster cap

Pilaster

Baluster

Newel post

Queen Anne Rowhouse

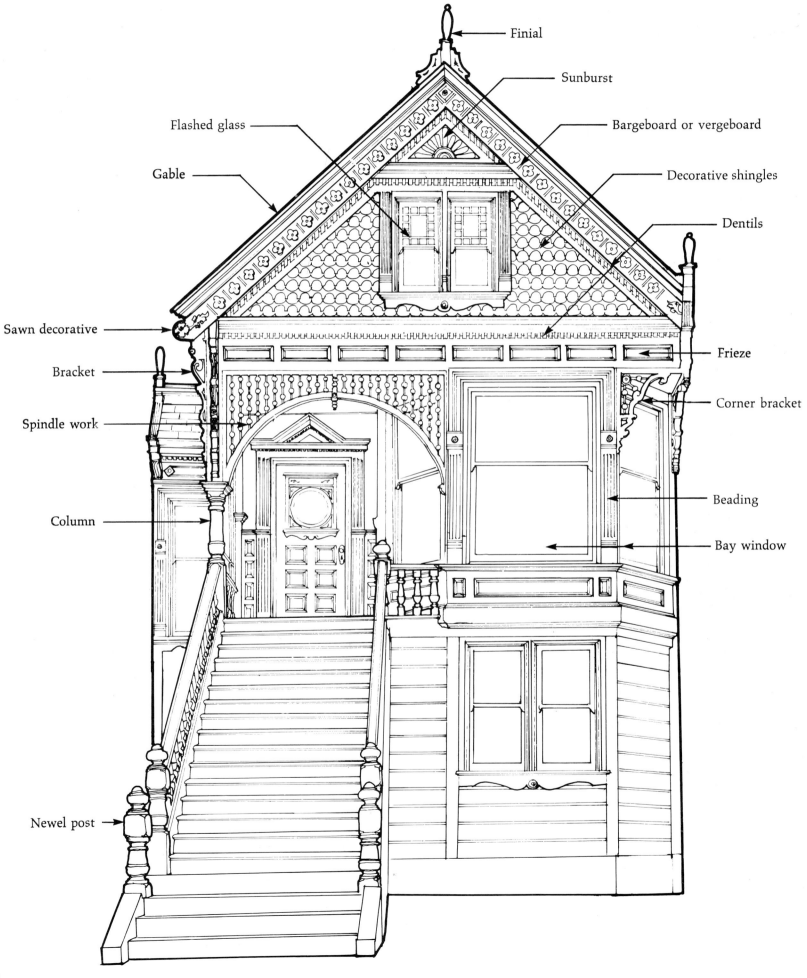

Finial

Sunburst

Flashed glass

Bargeboard or vergeboard

Gable

Decorative shingles

Dentils

Sawn decorative

Frieze

Bracket

Corner bracket

Spindle work

Beading

Column

Bay window

Newel post

Street Listing by Photograph Number

Photograph   Street
Number   Address

1. (cover) 3919 20th St.
2. 819 Eddy St.
3. 1839 Laguna St.
4. 506 East South Temple,
   Salt Lake City, Utah
   John E. Dooly Residence
5. 1341 Masonic St.
6. 317-19 Mississippi St.
7. 841-45 Fulton St.
8. 465-67 Oak St.
9. 2012-002 Pierce St.
10. 729-33 Shotwell St.
11. 733 Shotwell St.
12. 910 Shotwell St.
13. 1285-87 Dolores St.
14. 648-50 Capp St.
15. 926 Shotwell St.
16. 571-73 Liberty St.
17. 1278 Clayton St.
18. 145 Blake St.
19. 3603 26th St.
20. 1527 Jerold St.
21. 77-79 Hill St.
22. 1198 Fulton St.
23. 3243-45 21st St.
24. 3339-41 21st St.
25. 2107 Bush St.
26. 45 Lloyd St.
27. 807 Franklin St.
28. 274 Liberty St.
29. 6 Lloyd St.
30. 2339 Bryant St.
31. 125 Romain St.
32. 1757-59 Green St.
33. 1757-59 Green St.
34. 939-41 York St.
35. 939-41 York St.
36. 855 Hampshire St.
37. 1493-99 McAllister St.
38. 2026 California St.
39. 1013-15 Valencia St.
40. 1920 Golden Gate Ave.
41. 1427 Valencia St.
42. 807 Franklin St.
43. 725-27 Baker St.
44. 1037-41 Guerrero St.
45. 1201 Guerrero St.
46. 2619 Octavia St.
47. 9 Walter St.
48. 3751 23rd St.
49. 622 Spruce St.
50. 183 28th St.
51. 816 Douglass St.
52. 1728 Divisadero St.
53. 807 Franklin St.
54. 2307-09-11 California St.
55. 210 San Jose Ave.
56. 863 Guerrero St.
57. 1180-82 Guerrero St.
58. 214 Steiner St.
59. 1918 Pine St.
60. 1013-15 Valencia St.
61. 988 Valencia St.
62. 2385 Bush St.
63. 1838 Turk St.
64. 932 Shotwell St.
65. 881-87 Fulton St.
66. 609-13 Fell St.
67. 2255-57 Pine St.
68. 2255-57 Pine St.
69. 102 Guerrero St.
70. 102 Guerrero St.
71. 323-25 Haight St.
72. 323-25 Haight St.
73. 824 Grove St.
74. 824 Grove St.
75. 2018 California St.
76. 3933 23rd St.
77. 3901 Folsom St.
78. 604 Capp St.
79. 814 Hampshire St.
80. 718 Treat Ave.
81. 770-72 Treat Ave.
82. 2749-51 Bryant St.
83. 2442 Folsom St.
84. 4007-09 18th St.
85. 1619 Florida St.
86. 2906 Folsom St.
87. 1619 Florida St.
88. 807 Franklin St.
89. 3828 23rd St.
90. 772 South Van Ness Ave.
91. 2239-43 Pine St.
92. 148-58 Park St.
93. 284 Collingwood St.
94. 290 Collingwood St.
95. 59-61 Hill St.
96. 601 Broderick St.
97. 763 Turk St.
98. 1020 Shotwell St.
99. 1016-18 Shotwell St.
100. 1169 Valencia St.
101. 760-62 Treat Ave.
102. 986 Guerrero St.

103. 545 Sanchez St.
104. 4164-66 17th St.
105. 25 Hill St.
106. 1419 Webster St.
107. 3239-41 21st St.
108. 831-33 Hampshire St.
109. 1871 Green St.
110. 3380 23rd St.
111. 605-07 Haight St.
112. 321 Eureka St.
113. 1839 Laguna St.
114. 247-49 Webster St.
115. 1487-89 McAllister St.
116. 554 Hill St.
117. 884 Capp St.
118. 884 Capp St.
119. 884 Capp St.
120. 884 Capp St.
121. 5 Cottage Row
122. 3045-47 23rd St.
123. 2018 California St.
124. 811 Treat Ave.
125. 801-03 Clayton St.
126. 315 Castro St.
127. 917 Hampshire St.
128. 2615 California St.
129. 222-24 Hermann St.
130. 1040 Sanchez St.
131. 958-60 Capp St.
132. 2608 California St.
133. 3282 23rd St.
134. 1016 Pierce St.
135. 2101 Divisadero St.
136. 1016 Pierce St.
137. 814 Grove St.
138. 722-24 Fillmore St.
139. 856-58 Page St.
140. 711 Broderick St.
141. 77-79 Beaver St.
142. 1919-25 Greenwich St.
143. 4019-21 23rd St.
144. 413 Lyon St.
145. 224-26 Noe St.
146. 716 Steiner St.
147. 1690 Golden Gate Ave.
148. 809-11 Pierce St.
149. 2020 Golden Gate Ave.
150. 158 Downey St.
151. 2460 Folsom St.
152. 1671-73 McAllister St.
153. 1443-49 McAllister St.
154. 1618-16-14 Castro St.
155. 725 Castro St.
156. 1198 Fulton St.
157. 1812-14 Pacific Ave.
158. 642 Broderick St.
159. 809-11 Pierce St.
160. 809-11 Pierce St.
161. 809-11 Pierce St.
162. 809-11 Pierce St.
163. 809-11 Pierce St.
164. 1348 South Van Ness Ave.
165. 1348 South Van Ness Ave.
166. 1348 South Van Ness Ave.
167. 1348 South Van Ness Ave.
168. 1348 South Van Ness Ave.
169. 1348 South Van Ness Ave.
170. 623 Baker St.
171. 627 Baker St.
172. 3600 Washington St.
173. 3600 Washington St.
174. 145-47 Divisadero St.
175. 710 Broderick St.
176. 710 Steiner St.
177. 80 Caselli St.
178. 3441-43 20th St.
179. 597-99 Noe St.
180. 2000 Pacific Ave.
181. 263-65 Dolores St.
182. 924-34 Divisadero St.
183. 2004 Gough St.
184. 1493-99 McAllister St.
185. 1493-99 McAllister St.
186. 1834 California St.
187. 722-24 Fillmore St.
188. 722-24 Fillmore St.
189. 348-50 Scott St.
190. 348-50 Scott St.
191. 331-33 Lyon St.
192. 1247-51 Masonic St.
193. 853-57 Cole St.
194. 3845 21st St.
195. 1552 Palou Ave.
196. 2618 25th St.
197. 626 5th Ave.
198. 514 5th Ave.
199. 145-47 Cook St.
200. 860 Noe St.
201. 148 Buena Vista Ave.
202. 67 Delmar St.
203. 968 York St.
204. 982 York St.
205. 956 York St.
206. 968 Sanchez St.
207. 974 Sanchez St.
208. 261 2nd Ave.
209. 1451-53 McAllister St.
210. 2119 Bush St.
211. 1002 Noe St.
212. 477-79 Duboce Ave.
213. 1663 McAllister St.
214. 4331-33 20th St.
215. 1939 Oak St.
216. 707 Broderick St.
217. 1816 Church St.
218. 974 Sanchez St.
219. 1278 Clayton St.
220. 871 Hampshire St.
221. 56 Prosper St.
222. 1136 Potrero Ave.
223. 3845 21st St.
224. 945 Alabama St.
225. 3741 22nd St.
226. 854 Elizabeth St.

227. 957 Hampshire St.
228. 544 Hill St.
229. 23 Beaver St.
230. 556-58 Lyon St.
231. 410 Jersey St.
232. 859 Elizabeth St.
233. 559 Liberty St.
234. 217 Douglass St.
235. 171 Hartford St.
236. 417 Lyon St.
237. 545 Sanchez St.
238. 234-36 Noe St.
239. 345 Jersey St.
240. 197-99 Collingwood St.
241. 4156 20th St.
242. 217 Clipper St.
243. 4579-81 18th St.
244. 706 Wisconsin St.
245. 877 Alvarado St.
246. 957 Hampshire St.
247. 4535 19th St.
248. 207 Day St.
249. 197-99 Collingwood St.
250. 4049 18th St.
251. 597-99 Noe St.
252. 622 Spruce St.
253. 170 Highland Ave.
254. 158 Park St.
255. 2749-51 Bryant St.
256. 2468-70 Folsom St.
257. 1447-49 Valencia St.
258. 306 Shotwell St.
259. 62 Hattie St.
260. 1020 Shotwell St.
261. 421 Laurel St.
262. 268 6th Ave.
263. 1777 Page St.
264. 1326 Masonic St.
265. 116 Fair Oaks St.
266. 618-20 Haight St.
267. 3243-45 21st St.
268. 3243-45 21st St.
269. 3243-45 21st St.
270. 3243-45 21st St.
271. 3243-45 21st St.
272. 270 Liberty St.
273. 725 Treat Ave.
274. 3243-45 21st St.
275. 2774 California St.
276. 1265 Guerrero St.
277. 201 Downey St.
278. 309 Steiner St.
279. 442 Lyon St.
280. 1737 Webster St.
281. 1737 Webster St.
282. 1737 Webster St.
283. 1737 Webster St.
284. 1737 Webster St.
285. 300 Pennsylvania Ave.
286. 2712 Harrison St.
287. 745 Shotwell St.
288. 3675 16th St.

289. 1002-12 Tennessee St.
290. 2661-67 Harrison St.
291. 12-14 Webster St.
292. 1164 Church St.
293. 258 Fair Oaks St.
294. 516 Connecticut St.
295. 955-61 Valencia St.
296. 703-05-07 Shotwell St.
297. 510 Noe St.
298. 1652 Lyon St.
299. 201 Buchanan St.
300. 252-54 Downey St.
301. 1713 Green St.

Alphabetical Street Listing

Here is a list of the house photographs in *A Gift To The Street*, arranged alphabetically by street address. Numbered streets and avenues are at the end of the list.

Where it was available, we have included information about the origin of each house. Further research about builders, architects and construction dates is underway; therefore this list will be expanded in future editions.

KEY

( ) photograph number

WD — Water Connection Date. Not always an accurate guide to construction date, because many homes had private wells, and many tract houses were connected at once, even though individual houses were not completed until later. Despite the potential inaccuracies, the water department records are among the few still available which did not perish in San Francisco's 1906 fire.

O — original owner
A — Architect
B — Builder
C — Carpenter

945 Alabama St., (224).
877 Alvarado St., (245), WD = 1898, B = A. Nash.
623 Baker St., (170).
627 Baker St., (171).
725-27 Baker St., (43).
23 Beaver St., (229).
77-79 Beaver St., (141).
145 Blake St., (18), demolished.
601 Broderick St., (96).
642 Broderick St., (158).
707 Broderick St., (216).
710 Broderick St., (175).
711 Broderick St., (140).
2339 Bryant St., (30).
2749-51 Bryant St., (82, 255).
201 Buchanan St., (299), A = John Marquis.
148 Buena Vista Ave., (201).
2107 Bush St., (25), WD = 1874, O/B = C. L. Taylor.
2119 Bush St., (210), WD = 1874, O = T. C. Steele.
2385 Bush St., (62).
1834 California St., (186), built in 1876 for Isaac Wormser, San Francisco Landmark No. 53.
2018 Califorina St., (75, 123), WD = 1886, O = John Wieland.
2026 California St., (38), WD = 1878.
2307-11 California St., (54), WD = 1876, O = B. G. Allen.

2608 California St., (132).
2615 California St., (128), WD = 1892, O = Dr. Edward A. Selfridge.
2774 California St., (275).
604 Capp St., (78).
648-50 Capp St., (14).
884 Capp St., (117, 118, 119, 120).
958-60 Capp St., (131).
80 Caselli St., (177).
315 Castro St., (126).
725 Castro St., (155), WD = 1897, O = L. E. Meredith, B = Fernando Nelson.
1614-16-18 Castro St., (154), B = Fernando Nelson.
1164 Church St., (292).
1816 Church St., (217).
801-03 Clayton St., (125).
1278 Clayton St., (17, 219).
217 Clipper St., (242), WD = 1888-90, C = Frederick C. Kleebauer.
853-57 Cole St., (193).
197-99 Collingwood, St., (240, 249), WD = 1891.
284 Collingwood St., (93), WD = 1898, C = John A. Swenson. (Home had private well until 1898.)
290 Collingwood St., (94), WD = 1886, C = John A. Swenson.
145-47 Cook St., (199), WD = 1893.
516 Connecticut St., (294).

5 Cottage Row, (121), WD = 1882.
207 Day St., (248), WD = 1885, O = P. Frasher.
67 Delmar St., (202).
145-47 Divisadero St., (174).
924-34 Divisadero St., (182).
1728 Divisadero St., (52).
2101 Divisadero St., (135), WD = 1877, O = the Fotrell
family.
263-65 Dolores St., (181), WD = 1892.
1285-87 Dolores St., (13).
217 Douglass St., (234).
816 Douglass St., (51), C = Jonathan Anderson.
158 Downey St., (150).
201 Downey St., (277).
252-54 Downey St., (300).
477-79 Duboce Ave., (212).
819 Eddy St., (2), WD = 1880, O = Frederick D. Stadt-
muller, A = P. R. Schmidt, San Francisco
Landmark No. 35.
854 Elizabeth St., (226).
859 Elizabeth St., (232).
321 Eureka St., (112).
116 Fair Oaks St., (265).
258 Fair Oaks St., (293).
609-13 Fell St., (66).
722-24 Fillmore St., (138, 187, 188).
1619 Florida St., (85, 87).
2442 Folsom St., (83).
2460 Folsom St., (151).
2468 Folsom St., (256).
2906 Folsom St., (86).
3901 Folsom St., (77).
807 Franklin St., (27, 42, 53, 88), WD = 1870.
841-45 Fulton St., (7).
881-87 Fulton St., (65), WD = 1878.
1198 Fulton St., (22, 156), WD = 1889, A = Henry
Geilfuss, O = W. Westerfeld.
1690 Golden Gate Ave., (147).
1920 Golden Gate Ave., (40).
2020 Golden Gate Ave., (149).
2004 Gough St., (183), WD = 1889, O = Charles A.
Belden.
1713 Green St., (301).
1757-59 Green St., (32, 33).
1871 Green St., (109), WD = 1881.
1919-25 Greenwich St., (142), WD = 1890, O = D.
Samuels.
814 Grove St., (137), WD = 1882, O = Thomas
O'Connor.
824 Grove St., (73, 74), WD = 1886, O = Henry Brune.
102 Guerrero St., (69, 70).
863 Guerrero St., (56), WD = 1872, O = J. Mahoney.
986 Guerrero St., (102), A/O = Charles Geddes.
1037-41 Guerrero St., (44).
1180-82 Guerrero St., (57), WD = 1884.
1201 Guerrero St., (45).
1265 Guerrero St., (276).
323-25 Haight St., (71, 72).
605-07 Haight. St., (111).
618-20 Haight St., (266).
814 Hampshire St., (79).
831-33 Hampshire St., (108).

855 Hampshire St., (36).
871 Hampshire St., (220).
917 Hampshire St., (127).
957 Hampshire St., (227, 246).
2661-67 Harrison St., (290).
2712 Harrison St., (286).
171 Hartford St., (235), WD = 1895, O = Mike Dolan.
62 Hattie St., (259).
222-24 Hermann St., (129).
25 Hill St., (105), WD = 1885, O = J. F. Gaylor.
59-61 Hill St., (95), WD = 1882, O = J. W. Lunny.
77-79 Hill St., (21).
554 Hill St., (116, 228), WD = 1890, A/B = Isaac
Anderson.
170 Highland St., (253).
1527 Jerold St., (20).
345 Jersey St., (239).
410 Jersey St., (231).
1839 Laguna St., (3, 113), WD = 1887.
421 Laurel St., (261), WD = 1890.
270 Liberty St., (272).
274 Liberty St., (28).
559 Liberty St., (233), WD = 1897, B = Carlson and
Anderson.
551-73 Liberty St., (16), WD = 1897-8, B = Carlson and
Anderson, O = Alfred and Clara Ledeine.
6 Lloyd St., (29).
45 Lloyd St., (26).
331-33 Lyon St., (191).
413 Lyon St., (144).
417 Lyon St., (236).
442 Lyon St., (279).
556-58 Lyon St., (230).
1652 Lyon St., (298).
1247-51 Masonic St., (192).
1326 Masonic St., (264), B = W. Hamerton.
1341 Masonic St., (5).
1443-49 McAllister St., (153).
1451-53 McAllister St., (209).
1487-89 McAllister St., (115).
1493-99 McAllister St., (37, 184, 185).
1663 McAllister St., (213).
1671-73 McAllister St., (152).
317-19 Mississippi St., (6).
224-26 Noe St., (145).
234-36 Noe St., (238).
510 Noe.St., (297).
597-99 Noe St., (179, 251).
860 Noe St., (200).
1002 Noe St., (211).
465 Oak St., (8), WD = 1876.
1939 Oak St., (215), WD = 1895, O = John F. Shrodes.
2619 Octavia St., (46).
1812-14 Pacific Ave., (157), WD = 1891, O = Isaac
Liebes.
2000 Pacific Ave., (180), WD = 1894, O = Charles B.
York.
856-58 Page St., (139).
1777 Page St., (263), O/B = Robert D. Cranston.
1552 Palou Ave., (195).
148-58 Park St., (92).
158 Park St., (254).

300 Pennsylvania Ave., (285), WD = 1868, O = Capt.
Charles Adams.
809-11 Pierce St., (148, 159, 160, 161, 162, 163).
WD = 1894, O = William McCormick.
1016 Pierce St., (134, 136), WD = 1886.
2002-12 Pierce St., (9).
1918 Pine St., (59), WD = 1876.
2239-43 Pine St., (91), WD = 1871, O = B. Leavy.
2255-57 Pine St., (67, 68).
1136 Potrero Ave., (222).
56 Prosper St., (221), WD = 1888, O = S. L. Merrill.
125 Romain St., (31).
545 Sanchez St., (103, 237), WD = 1889, O = Richard
Miller.
968 Sanchez St., (206), WD = 1891, C = James T.
McInnes.
974 Sanchez St., (207, 218), WD = 1891, C = James T.
McInnes.
1040 Sanchez St., (130), WD = 1896, O = Mrs. B.
Sexton.
210 San Jose Ave., (55), WD = 1878, O/C = John
Greenwood.
348-50 Scott St., (189, 190), WD = 1890, O = Harry W.
Lohsen.
306 Shotwell St., (258).
703-05-07 Shotwell St., (296).
729-33 Shotwell St., (10).
733 Shotwell St., (11).
745 Shotwell St., (287).
910 Shotwell St., (12).
926 Shotwell St., (15).
932 Shotwell St., (64).
1016-18 Shotwell St., (99).
1020 Shotwell St., (98, 260).
772 South Van Ness Ave., (90).
1348 South Van Ness Ave., (164 through 169), WD =
1886, A = Seth Bobson, O = Frank M. Stone,
San Francisco Landmark No. 74.
622 Spruce St., (49, 252).
214 Steiner St., (58).
309 Steiner St., (278).
710 Steiner St., (176), WD = 1894, B = Matthew
Kavanagh.
716 Steiner St., (146), WD = 1895, B = Matthew
Kavanagh.
1002-12 Tennessee St., (289).
718 Treat Ave., (80).
725 Treat Ave., (273).
760-62 Treat Ave., (101).
770-72 Treat Ave., (81).
811 Treat Ave., (124), WD = 1883, A/O = Henry
Geilfuss.
763 Turk St., (97), WD = 1889.
1838 Turk St., (63).
955, 959-61 Valencia St., (295).
988 Valencia St., (61).
1013-15 Valencia St., (39, 60).
1169 Valencia St., (100).
1427 Valencia St., (41), WD = 1898, B = Joseph Flood,
O = John A. Christen.
1447-49 Valencia St., (257), WD = 1889, O = John
Creamer.

9 Walter St., (47).
3600 Washington St., (172, 173), WD = 1897.
247-49 Webster St., (114).
412-14 Webster St., (291).
1419 Webster St., (106).
1737 Webster St., (280 through 284), A = Newsom
Brothers.
706 Wisconsin St., (244).
939-41 York St., (34, 35).
956 York St., (205).
968 York St., (203).
982 York St., (204).

Numbered Streets and Avenues

261 2nd Ave., (208).
514 5th Ave., (198).
626 5th Ave., (197), WD = 1906-07, B = Fernando
Nelson.
268 6th Ave., (262).
3675 16th St., (288).
4164-66 17th St., (104).
4007-09 18th St., (84).
4049 18th St., (250).
4579-81 18th St., (243).
4535 19th St., (247).
3441-43 20th St., (178), WD = 1891, O = George Henry
Richard.
3919-21 20th St., (1–Cover).
4156 20th St., (241).
4331-33 20th St., (214), WD = 1891.
3239-41 21st St., (107), WD = 1885, O = C. Rohrig.
3243-45 21st St., (23, 267 through 271, 274).
3339-41 21st St., (24), WD = 1876, C = James
Kavanagh.
3845 21st St., (194, 223), WD = 1896, O = Charles Rolf.
3741 22nd St., (225), WD = 1897, B = Hans Petersen.
3045-47 23rd St., (122).
3282 23rd St., (133).
3380 23rd St., (110).
3751 23rd St., (48), WD = 1890, O = James M. Ward.
3828 23rd St., (89).
3933 23rd St., (76), WD = 1891, O = J. Israel.
4019-21 23rd St., (143).
2618 25th St., (196).
3603 26th St., (19).
183 28th St., (50).

Index

Advertisements, Illustrations 7, 8, 9
Balloon Frame Construction, pp. 148-9, Illustration 6 in Appendix
Bathroom, Illustration 28
Bay window, Illustration 27
Bicknell, A.J., p. 165
California Architect and Building News, pp. 147, 150-2, Illustration 4
Centennial Exposition, pp. 147, 164, 168
"Cheap Dwellings," pp. 171-3
Combined stool and bustle, p. 147, Illustration 5
Comstock, William, pp. 165-6
Eastlake, Charles Locke, pp. 164-5, 167-8
"Eastlake" furniture, p. 167
"Eastlake" house plans, pp. 165-7, Illustrations 37 through 41
"Eastlake" metallic shingles, Illustration 36
"Gingerbread," p. 168
Hints on Household Taste, pp. 164-5
Horton, George King, pp. 156-7, Illustrations 29, 30
House plans, pp. 147-156, Illustrations 2, 10 through 23, 37 through 42, 44 through 49
Interior designs, Illustrations 25 through 27
Johns-Manville asbestos shingles, p. 174, photograph 295
Joost Brothers, p. 165
Lot size, p. 170
Machinery, pp. 147-9, Illustrations 7, 8
Misguided improvements, pp. 173-4, photographs 295, 296, 297
Moorish divan, Illustration 26
Niehaus Brothers Planing Mill, p. 159, Illustration 32
Nelson, Fernando, pp. 70, 157-9, 162, Illustration 31
Newel post, Illustration 24
Newsom Brothers, p. 166
Paint colors, pp. 163, 168
Pelton, John Jr., pp. 171-2
Permastone, p. 174, photograph 297
Philadelphia Centennial Exposition, pp. 147, 164, 168
Queen Anne, pp. 164, 168-70
Queen Victoria, p. 164
Salfield, David, p. 166
Salvage, p. 173
San Francisco Victoriana, p. 174
Scientific American Architects and Builders Edition, pp. 147, 151, Illustration 3
Sidewalk plates, p. xv. See also photographs throughout book.
Signature details, pp. xv, 49, 159
Stucco, p. 174, photograph 296
Styles, pp. 163-70, Appendix drawings pp. 180, 181, 182, 183, 184
Textured coating, p. 174
Tower, pp. 74, 169-70, Illustrations 23, 45, 48
Townley Brothers, p. 159
Western Platform Framing, p. 148

Illustration Sources

1. *California Architect and Building News* (CABN), August, 1886.
2. CABN, January, 1880.
3. *Scientific American Architects and Builders Edition* (SA), June, 1885.
4. CABN, October, 1883.
5. SA, February, 1887.
6. Balloon-framing sequence, prepared by Stephen Rynerson.
7. SA, January, 1888.
8. SA, January, 1891.
9. Dunham, Carrigan and Co., hardware, CABN, December, 1880; The Day Mfg. Co., portable folding bathtub, SA, July, 1890; W. H. Mullins, Stamped Ornaments, SA, July, 1890; Lidell and Williams, Base, Head and Corner Blocks, SA, January, 1891; W. H. Mullins, Architectural Sheet Metal, SA, July, 1892.
10. SA, March, 1892.
11. SA, December, 1886.
12. SA, July, 1891.
13. CABN, October, 1883.
14. CABN, December, 1885.
15. CABN, February, 1882.
16. SA, January, 1887.
17. SA, October, 1887.
18. CABN, December, 1886.
19. CABN, April, 1880.
20. CABN, November, 1881.
21. CABN, May, 1885.
22. SA, November, 1887.
23. SA, January, 1890.
24. SA, May, 1887.
25. SA, December, 1890.
26. SA, February, 1894.
27. SA, August, 1893.
28. SA, May, 1901.
29. George King Horton photograph, courtesy of George H. Horton.
30. Frontispiece of Horton Diary, courtesy of George H. Horton.
31. George and Fernando Nelson with fire officials, 1906, courtesy of the Nelson family.
32. Niehaus Brothers catalogue pages, courtesy of San Francisco Victoriana.
33. SA, January, 1892.
34. SA, July, 1894.
35. SA, July, 1896.
36. SA, October, 1887.
37. CABN, October, 1881.
38. CABN, October, 1881.
39. CABN, October, 1881.
40. CABN, December, 1881.
41. SA, May, 1887.
42. CABN, September, 1886.
43. SA, August, 1896.
44. CABN, September, 1884.
45. CABN, August, 1885.
46. CABN, July, 1880.
47. CABN, February, 1880.
48. SA, October, 1890.

References

The opening and closing quote of this book is from the Navaho House Dedication Ceremony, "Navaho Houses," C. Mindeleff, *Seventeenth Annual Report of the U.S. Bureau of American Ethnology, 1895-96*, Government Printing Office, 1898, Part 2, pp. 504-5.

1. From *Selected Prose of Robert Frost* edited by Hyde Cox and Edward Connery Lathem. Copyright 1939, 1954, (c) 1966, 1967 by Holt, Rinehart and Winston. Copyright 1946, (c) 1959 by Robert Frost. Copyright (c) 1956 by The Estate of Robert Frost. Reprinted by permission of Holt, Rinehart and Winston, Publishers.
2. *Domestic Architecture*, Francis Goodwin, H. G. Bohn: London, 1850.
3. *Victorian Inventions*, Leonard de Vries, compiler, American Heritage Press, 1972.
4. *The Tastemakers*, Russell Lynes, Universal Library, Grosset and Dunlap: New York, 1972, pp. 112-117.
5. *California's Architectural Frontier*, Harold Kirker, Peregrine Smith, Inc: Santa Barbara, 1973. *Carpentry*, Book I, William S. Lowndes, International Textbook Company: Philadelphia, 1933, pp. 2-36.
6. "Origins of the Balloon Frame", Walker Field, *Journal of the Society of Architectural Historians*, October, 1946.
7. *California Architect and Building News* (CABN), November, 1880, p. 105.
8. *Scientific American Architects and Builders Edition* (SA), March, 1892, p. 47.
9. SA, August, 1892, p. 79.
10. CABN, January, 1880, p. 1.
11. CABN, January, 1894, p. 1.
12. CABN, December, 1880, p. 114.
13. CABN, April, 1884, p. 64.
14. *San Francisco Real Estate Circular*, October, 1883.
15. Diary excerpts and illustrations courtesy of George H. Horton.
16. Information about Fernando Nelson was compiled from personal interviews with family, from newspaper articles and from Nelson's receipt books.
17. *San Francisco Chronicle*, June 19, 1887, p. 13.
18. *ibid.*
19. *Specimen Book of One Hundred Architectural Designs*, A.J. Bicknell and Company: New York, 1878.
20. *San Francisco Chronicle*, June 21, 1887.
21. CABN, October, 1885, p. 180; SA, October, 1887, p. 81.
22. *Hints on Household Taste*, Charles Locke Eastlake, reprinted in *Late Victorian Decor*, American Life Foundation: New York, 1968.
23. *Modern Architectural Designs and Details*, William T. Comstock, Architectural Publisher: New York, 1881, plate 71. Note: This catalogue was reproduced in 1975, by the American Life Foundation: *Victorian Architecture, Two Pattern Books*.
24. *Late Victorian Decor*, p. 118.
25. CABN, October, 1881, plate 4, p. 103.
26. CABN, October, 1881, plates 2 and 3, p. 103.
27. CABN, December, 1881, plate 1, p. 128.
28. SA, May, 1887, p. 105.
29. CABN, October, 1881, p. 97.
30. CABN, April, 1882, p. 49.
31. CABN, April, 1883, p. 54.
32. CABN, September, 1886, p. 135.
33. CABN, February, 1883, p. 25.
34. SA, December, 1891, p. 88.
35. SA, January, 1892, p. 2.
36. SA, February, 1892, p. 14.
37. SA, June, 1896, p. 83.
38. SA, September, 1895, p. 149.
39. CABN, June, 1883, p. 90.
40. CABN, September, 1884, p. 157-8.
41. SA, January, 1903, p. 2.
42. SA, March, 1902, p. 43.
43. *San Francisco Evening Bulletin*, April 3, 1880.
44. CABN, April, 1880, p. 38.
45. *San Francisco Evening Bulletin*, May 8, 1880.
46. CABN, June, 1880, p. 52.
47. CABN, August, 1880, p. 73.
48. CABN, July, 1880, p. 68.
49. CABN, December, 1880, p. 116.
50. *San Francisco Evening Bulletin*, April, 1883.
51. CABN, May, 1883, p. 76.
52. SA, October, 1897, p. 57.
53. SA, August, 1900, pp. 22-23.
54. SA, July, 1901, p. 17.
55. *American Carpenter and Builder*, February, 1916, p. 38.
56. Survey conducted by Judith Waldhorn, Fall, 1975.

Final quote at the end of the text section on page 175 is taken from "Two", *Tao Te Ching*, Lao Tsu, translated by Gia-fu Feng and Jane English, Alfred A. Knopf, Inc: New York. Copyright 1972. Reprinted with the permission of the publisher.

A Very Special Thank You to . . .

Mel Kranke, for being one of the most honest, kind, decent, hardworking individuals in the state of California, and for not laughing when, after selling me a 35mm camera, a view camera, meter, tripod, etc., he realized I didn't know a shutter speed from an f stop.

Dominic DiMare, for being a continual spring of original ideas, useful criticisms, wild suggestions and just plain invaluable help.

Richard Schuettge, for saying what he did and doing what he said, and for his willingness to work, suggest, criticize, allow, and to take a chance.

Judith Waldhorn, for her enthusiasm and generosity, and for simply being a wonderful person to work with.

Stephen Rynerson, the maker of the balloon construction and Victorian house drawings, for his fine draftsmanship and his patience in working with me.

Emahmn, for his wisdom, support, advice and good company during the photographing for this book.

Diane Orr, my most wonderfully unsensible of friends, who thought this documentation project a sensible thing to do and who encouraged me to do it when no one else did, for her eternal optimism, intelligence, and adventurous spirit.

Terri Bohac, for having weathered this project with her characteristic kindness, consideration and good humor.

Larry Tuft, for his generous loan of darkroom equipment.

Frederick Mitchell, for being the only person in the publishing world to offer any encouragement in the early stages of this book, and for his willingness to be pestered for advice.

Stewart Emery, for his suggestions on how to make the doing of this book a joy.

The people at San Francisco Victoriana, for their inspiration on what can be done if you care.

My friends whom I have not already mentioned, for their warmth, encouragement, trust and support.

And finally, to the people of San Francisco whom I met on the streets, and most especially the children and the older people who for two years were my daily companions, and who shared with me their thoughts, stories, questions and songs — moments of themselves.

From Carol

The many people who have given me sustenance in my work. It would be impossible to thank them all for inviting me to their homes and sharing their thoughts, memories and old house revivals. I would, however, like to mention some cherished friends and colleagues whose assistance was essential:

The restoration firm of San Francisco Victoriana, whose careful craftsmanship and high standards show that authentic reconstruction of Victorian homes is an achievable art. I would especially like to thank Gary Kray, co-founder and partner of Victoriana.

The staffs at these libraries: California Room, California State Library in Sacramento; the California Historical Society in San Francisco; the Museum of History and Technology of the Smithsonian Institution in Washington, D.C., the San Francisco Main Public Library, and the Library of Congress in Washington, D.C.

For permission to use quotations, photographs and illustrations: SCIENTIFIC AMERICAN, New York; George H. Horton, for letting me use photographs and diary excerpts from his grandfather, George King Horton; Mrs. Janet Post and her father, George R. Nelson, and Penny de Paoli, who introduced us to Mr. Nelson.

These people gave me their professional support and judgments: Merrill Ware, National Endowment for the Arts; Gladys Hansen, San Francisco City Archivist, and Pat Akre, her assistant; Kevin Starr, former San Francisco City Librarian; Richard Hedman and George Williams, San Francisco Department of City Planning; and Knox Mellon, Director of the Office of Historic Preservation, California State Department of Parks and Recreation.

Jim Paul and Anna Gussgard helped me with the 1500-block survey of San Francisco Victorian neighborhoods, and Miss Gussgard typed the manuscript for this text.

Finally, these people, whose enthusiasm helped me persist in tedious field work and in dusty archives: Bernadine Barr, Sally Bush, Delma Chuchwar, "The Crabtrees" (Bill, Mae, Marcia, Gary, Andy, Shon, Heidi, and Ginger), Luisa Ezquerro, Marge and Tom Filcich, Ellis and Jennifer Gans, Jim Haas, Jim Holloran, Butch and Karen Kardum, Anne Kelley, Max Kirkeberg, Jeremy Kotas, Toby Levine, Betty de Losada, Hal Major, Linda Marks, Pam McGuire, John Merritt, Ed Morse, Mrs. David Mosby, Barbara Norris, Dave Peterson, Julian Pichel, Else Reisner, Roger Scharmer, Laura Smith, Nan Warren, Christen Wegener, Shirryl Wilson, and Sally Woodbridge.

Finally, I would like to thank my husband, Steven, for his patience and for trying to learn to like old houses.

From Judith